GROVELAND AND BIG OAK FLAT

IMAGES of America

Two men are pictured next to their rifles with friends and family atop a vehicle around the 1910s. The animal pelt hanging from a pole appears to be a fox, which was a frequent hunting target in southern Tuolumne County in that era. Although the hand-lettered signs are partially obscured, they seem to provide a good-natured warning to anyone wanting to use the vehicle: "Don't call me . . . because am missing . . . four wheels, no brakes, dangerous, but passable." The wheel rims with no tires suggest that the warning was well justified. (Carlo M. De Ferrari Archive.)

ON THE COVER: In 1872, twenty-five-year-old James Mecartea converted a stone dwelling into this blacksmith shop just southwest of "the Divide," a ridge with an elevation of 3,090 feet that divides Big Oak Flat from Groveland. Austin, one of James and wife Elvira's 13 children, took ownership after his father's death in 1899. The business flourished until motorcars replaced horse transport by the early 1930s. Its stone walls and iron doors stood abandoned until the early 1980s, when it was torn down. (Mecartea Family Collection.)

IMAGES of America
GROVELAND AND BIG OAK FLAT

Southern Tuolumne County Historical Society
Foreword by Conrad Anker

Copyright © 2020 by the Southern Tuolumne County Historical Society
ISBN 978-1-4671-0528-6

Published by Arcadia Publishing
Charleston, South Carolina

Printed in the United States of America

Library of Congress Control Number: 2020934441

For all general information, please contact Arcadia Publishing:
Telephone 843-853-2070
Fax 843-853-0044
E-mail sales@arcadiapublishing.com
For customer service and orders:
Toll-Free 1-888-313-2665

Visit us on the Internet at www.arcadiapublishing.com

We dedicate this book to Southern Tuolumne County Historical Society founders, whose early commitment to preserving and promoting our local history led to the creation of our museum and ultimately this book.

Contents

Foreword ... 6

Acknowledgments ... 7

Introduction ... 8

1. First People ... 11
2. In Search of Gold ... 17
3. Traveling the Big Oak Flat Road ... 29
4. They Lived on the Hill ... 45
5. Making Ends Meet ... 57
6. Day to Day ... 69
7. Roadside History ... 83
8. Headquartering Hetch Hetchy ... 97
9. A Lasting Boom ... 111

Bibliography ... 126

About the Southern Tuolumne County Historical Society ... 127

Foreword

It is with thanks to the Southern Tuolumne County Historical Society that this book is making the history of the Groveland and Big Oak Flat area available to all.

We are born into this world with no hand in our destiny. That our parents would come together and share their genes is life's biggest luck of the draw. We begin breathing with their physical embodiments and mature with their love and vision. Our upbringing is based on our surroundings.

My father, Wally Anker, was always proud of his roots at Priest Station, even though the sand in his shoes took him around the world. His bride, my mother Helga, left her place of birth to be part of Tuolumne County. As founding members of Southern Tuolumne County Historical Society, they realized well that knowledge of one's local area and community are helpful in finding one's place in life. They both worked hard to establish the Groveland Yosemite Gateway Museum, dedicated to an appreciation of the past and the enjoyment and enlightenment of all who visit.

Place and its environment define how our ancestors interacted with fellow humans. While much of this might seem superfluous to the modern person in today's hyperconnected digital world, there is figurative gold in the understanding and appreciation of those that came before us.

There is an appreciation and respect for those that came before us that is reflected by honoring their passage with history. For this act of dedication, I am most grateful to the people of southern Tuolumne County.

—Conrad Anker, January 2020
Climber, mountaineer, author
Son of Southern Tuolumne County Historical Society
founders Helga and Wally Anker

Acknowledgments

The Southern Tuolumne County Historical Society (STCHS) sincerely thanks Scott Belser and Kathy Brown, Arcadia project coordinators, who devoted many volunteer hours to selecting photographs and writing text for this book. Our praise goes to Bob Oakley, who skillfully prepared the images for publication.

We are very grateful to Karen Davis for researching requested chapter topics and suggesting captions; Dave Gookin and Jim Phillips for freely sharing their personal knowledge of the area; Conrad Anker for writing our foreword even while adventuring in Antarctica; Dodie Harte and Kathy Seaton for advising on initial procedures; Bruce and Carrie Carter for researching and writing past articles about local buildings; Denise Henderson for providing past photograph captioning information; and all past volunteers in the STCHS History Research Center and former curators for amassing the information and photographs that form the basis for this book.

We thank the Carlo M. De Ferrari Archive and archivist Andy Mattos, the Tuolumne County Museum Archive and curator Billie Lyons, and Pine Mountain Lake Association and administrative assistant Debra Durai for aiding in the search for Groveland-area photographs and providing digital copies.

Our appreciation goes to the STCHS Arcadia Committee and Board for its business decisions and input regarding this project and especially to Pres. Harriet Codeglia, who has helped, advised, and encouraged us every step of the way.

Finally, we are grateful to the families of those working on the project, who wholeheartedly supported and sustained our efforts, and to those families in our area who shared their historic photographs with us through the years. Without their generosity and awareness of the importance of preserving our area's history, this book would not be possible.

All images not otherwise noted are courtesy of STCHS archives. Photographs credited in captions to donating local families are also a part of the STCHS archives unless otherwise noted. Abbreviations used in photograph credits are HHPC (Hetch Hetchy Photo Collection) and PMLA (Pine Mountain Lake Association).

INTRODUCTION

For thousands of years, only the Me-Wuk people lived in the central foothills of the Sierra Nevada, the location of Big Oak Flat and Groveland. They lived in small villages below the mountain heights and traded goods with neighboring tribes. Wild animals and native plants provided them with food, shelter, and medicines. Evidence of their way of life can be seen in bedrock mortar stones, arrowheads, woven baskets, and other artifacts found in the areas where they once lived.

The peaceful culture of the Me-Wuk people was negatively impacted and changed forever by the arrival of other cultures in California. In 1769, the Spanish appeared. Others of European origin arrived from the eastern United States in the early 1800s. Settlers established ranches and commercial stations along the coast and in the nearby Central Valley.

In January 1848, gold was discovered in the Sierra foothills, and the news spread quickly around the world. By the next year, gold seekers, known as forty-niners, from the Americas, Europe, and Asia began to flood into what would become the state of California in 1850. The California Gold Rush had begun.

At this time, James Savage, who was present at the first gold strike at Coloma, near Sacramento, set off to find gold in less crowded places. As he moved south through the California foothills, he established relationships with the indigenous people, learned their languages, and often married women from the local groups, thus creating political alliances with area tribes. He established a trading post in each new gold camp to which he moved. He sold picks, shovels, and other goods to the arriving miners. While at the Woods Creek gold strike in Jamestown, he learned from the Me-Wuk that there was gold in the foothills south of the Tuolumne River. In 1849, Savage established a productive gold-mining camp, including a trading post, near the top of a steep grade out of the Tuolumne River valley. The camp was on a gold-laden stream later named Rattlesnake Creek. As word of the new strike got out, more prospectors quickly arrived. The miners expanded eastward in search of gold and formed other mining camps along the creeks in the area. Collectively, these camps became known as "Savage's Diggings." It is believed that Savage's trading post near Rattlesnake Creek was on or near the site of the Wells Fargo (Gamble) building, which was completed in 1852 and is still standing today.

In 1850, when the area became crowded with miners and the easy gold was gone, Savage left to establish another gold camp and trading post farther south on the Merced River. The town that formed around the area he had left was named Big Oak Flat in honor of a massive oak tree that grew there. A smaller camp to the east became known as Garrote, the Spanish word for "hanging." This form of swift frontier justice, imposed upon lawbreakers, was practiced in the town in its earliest days.

At that time, prospecting in the area took the form of placer mining—finding gold near the surface of the ground or in creeks and rivers. Gold was plentiful in the area. Hopeful miners arrived in great numbers and panned for gold standing elbow to elbow along the local water sources. Some miners did strike it rich. However, for many, life in the gold camps was difficult. The easy gold was quickly exhausted, and the area streams were seasonal. Rattlesnake Creek dried up in the summer. There was only enough water to mine effectively in the winter and rainy spring season, meaning that the men panned and sluiced for gold most of the time while standing in ice-cold streams. Disease, accidents, drought, disappointment, and violence were all too common for the prospectors.

The biggest difficulty of the 1850s seemed to be overcome by 1860. In that year, a 36-mile-long water ditch was completed. The Golden Rock Ditch brought water from the South Fork of the Tuolumne River near Harden Flat via ditch, flume, and inverted siphon to Garrote and Big Oak Flat. Hotels, liveries, restaurants, and saloons were opened. The town of Big Oak Flat, the richer and bigger of the two camps on the hill, thrived in the late 1850s and incorporated to formally become a town. The population was estimated to be several thousand, and it had about 200 buildings, among them four hotels and a brick theater. It competed with Sonora to become the county seat. The population was very diverse, with a Chinese community, Mexicans, Bolivians, Hawaiians, and people from all over Europe. Many of the pioneer families of southern Tuolumne County came from Northern Italy and Ireland. Stages ran from Chinese Camp to Big Oak Flat and Garrote daily. Goods were paid for in gold dust or nuggets. However, a drought brought this boom to a sudden halt when a disastrous fire began in the evening of October 25, 1863, that nearly destroyed Big Oak Flat entirely.

By the 1870s, the early gold-mining era was over. While there was still some mining, the principal activity became ranching. Big Oak Flat, which was never able to fully recover from the 1863 fire, was disincorporated in 1864.

Road travel had been possible since the 1850s by stage or wagon from the boat docks in Stockton to Big Oak Flat. It was also possible to reach Chinese Camp to the west by train in 1897. The first signs of tourism in the Groveland area were seen with the completion of the Big Oak Flat Toll Road in 1874. It allowed travelers to make the trip the rest of the way to Yosemite Valley. New hotels, restaurants, and stage services were needed to serve the traveler. A series of wayside stations were developed to fulfill the demands along the way.

In 1875, when the town of Garrote changed its name to Groveland, it symbolized the end of the rough-and-ready Gold Rush days. Tuolumne County became more peaceful, and many families arrived to join those miners who chose to stay in the area. The arrival of those families, along with other relatives and friends, necessitated the building of new homes, stores, and schools.

In the 1890s, a new technology, deep-shaft mining, brought a renewed gold boom to Big Oak Flat and Groveland. Deep mines were dug, and stamp mills were constructed on the hillsides just off the main road behind both areas. The din of the mills filled the air throughout the town as they ran day and night to crush ore taken from the mines to extract the gold. However, even the new technology could not stop the depletion of the ore supply, and mining activity declined sharply in the 1920s.

Automobiles began to make an appearance in the early 1900s, and with them came the need for better roads. Of major importance to the region was the building of New Priest Grade to enable cars to climb to the top of Priest Hill (also known as Moccasin Hill).

An entirely new phase of development began in 1915 with the undertaking of the Hetch Hetchy project to impound and transport water from the Sierras to San Francisco. To bring water to the city, a dam impounding the Tuolumne River and 160 miles of water-transporting tunnels had to be built. The City of San Francisco also built a 68-mile-long railroad to transport heavy equipment, cement, and other materials as well as the men needed to build the dam in the Hetch Hetchy Valley of Yosemite. San Francisco chose Groveland, just 20 miles west of the dam being built in the wilderness, to serve as the administrative headquarters. For the next 10 years, the Groveland area benefited from being at the center of a project with hundreds of workers, engineers, suppliers, and supporting staff. The old railyard and maintenance area for the project can still be seen near the Groveland museum and library, where an administrative center for the project was located.

After the completion of the O'Shaughnessey Dam and the Mountain Tunnel section of the aqueduct, the buildings of the administrative center in Groveland and the railroad were dismantled. Workers left to find jobs constructing the aqueduct farther down the line or elsewhere. The area once again fell into a quiet time of timber mills and ranching, and with only a few hundred residents in the area, businesses closed.

In 1969, an essential boost was given when the Boise Cascade Corporation chose the area just east of Groveland's Main Street to build a new vacation community. It offered a man-made lake, a golf course, and a small airstrip. Hundreds of homes were built along newly created streets on forested hillsides. That development, called Pine Mountain Lake, now counts a population of about 3,000 people.

In the 21st century, Groveland and Big Oak Flat have seen steady growth in tourism. State Highway 120 follows the nearly 150-year-old Big Oak Flat Road to Yosemite. It is the northern gateway to Yosemite and the fastest road to the national park from the San Francisco Bay Area. The Stanislaus National Forest surrounding the area also provides many recreational opportunities. Each year brings more tourists and facilities to the highway and more opportunities to enjoy the region's unique combination of history, recreation, and natural wonders.

One

First People

The Me-Wuk people have inhabited the Sierra foothills for several thousand years. Proof of their encampments is found in bedrock mortars, grinding stones, and other artifacts discovered in the area.

Prior to the Gold Rush, the Me-Wuk lived in balance with nature, which supplied all their needs. Plentiful game, fish, grasses, and minimal snow made the area ideal for establishing camps. An abundance of oak trees provided acorns, the year-round staple of their diet. They traded acorns and baskets with other tribal groups to provide for some of their other needs, such as shells, salt, pine nuts, and obsidian.

The Me-Wuk way of life changed rapidly and forever with arrival of miners who infringed upon their lands. Many of their harvesting grounds for bulbs, seed grasses, and berries were stripped bare by gold-seekers or trampled by grazing. Rivers, their source of fish and hygiene, were polluted by mining practices. The oaks that were their year-round source of staple food were cleared. They died from introduced diseases to which they had no immunity. The Sierra Me-Wuk population was drastically reduced from 10,000 prior to outside contact to less than 700 in 1910.

Me-Wuk camps were scattered all around the Big Oak Flat–Groveland area. Pigliku, also called Big Creek Rancheria because of its location, was one of the larger Me-Wuk sites. Pictures of Pigliku's ceremonial roundhouse are found in early printed archeological studies. In the band's final years at this site, their chief was Nomasu, also called Captain Louie. His daughter Sophia followed him as leader for a brief period.

With their land usurped, resources defiled, and numbers reduced to less than 20 at Big Creek in 1917, the few remaining Me-Wuk left Pigliku in 1922. Some went to the federally designated Tuolumne Rancheria near Tuolumne City. In 1970, their Big Creek Rancheria was inundated by the dammed waters of Big Creek, which now form Pine Mountain Lake. Me-Wuk continue to live in the area practicing their cultural and spiritual lifeways while integrating modern society.

Acorns provided a staple food for the Me-Wuk people. They dried and stored the nuts of the oak tree, unshelled, in granaries called *chuck-ah*, shown in this 1875 photograph. The storehouses were constructed of sticks loosely woven around poles and lined with grasses that repelled insects. The twigs were pushed apart so acorns could pour out when needed. Tannic acid in the acorns preserved them. (Yosemite National Park Archives.)

Grinding stones with cupped depressions, like this one in Big Oak Flat, are found in exposed bedrock scattered around the Groveland area. Generations of Me-Wuk women used the holes to pound seeds and nuts, especially acorns. They gathered at the mortars, using a rock pestle to pound shelled acorns into a fine meal. With use, what started as a dimple in the rock became larger and deeper.

The woman in this 1924 photograph by Edward Curtis is sifting the acorn meal that was ground in the bedrock mortars. Any meal not ground finely enough went back into the grinding hole. The acorn flour, caught in the weft of the woven basket, was leached with water to remove the tannins that made it bitter. (Library of Congress.)

After leaching, the acorn flour was mixed with water and cooked in woven baskets. White-hot stones from the fire were added to the mixture as needed until it thickened to make *nü'ppa* (soup), *yo'kko* (mush), or *u'lē* (bread). Acorns provided food even when weather was too inclement to hunt or forage. (California State University, Chico, Miriam Library Special Collections.)

Me-Wuk men fished and hunted to supply food for the tribe. Rainbow trout were often speared as they swam in the water. Fish in low-water pools were sometimes stunned using crushed soaproot. Deer and small game were hunted and often dried for a later supply of food. Animal pelts and hides were used for clothing and blankets. (Library of Congress.)

The *u-ma-cha* (bark house) in this late-1800s George Fiske photograph was the winter home of the Me-Wuk in the foothills. It was made of cedar poles interwoven with willow or grape vines and overlaid with slabs of cedar bark. A fire made in a dirt depression was used for inside warmth and cooking. Smoke escaped where the poles met at the top. (Yosemite National Park Archives.)

A ceremonial roundhouse or *hangi* existed at the Big Creek Rancheria in Groveland. It was used for hand games as well as harvest and mourning dances. In keeping with tradition, it was burned in 1893 upon the death of Big Creek's chief, Nomasu. A new roundhouse, pictured here, was then built. It was gone by 1922, when the few remaining Me-Wuk left Pigliku. (University of California, Berkeley.)

At ceremonial dances, Me-Wuk men might wear costumes such as this. The headdress was usually an extended band of red-shafted flicker feathers bound with sinew. A shoulder cape of eagle or hawk feathers and the pelt of a wild animal was also worn. Ceremonies reenacted history and myths and celebrated events such as the coming of age of youths and the acorn festival. (California State University, Chico, Meriam Library Special Collections.)

This is the only photograph thought to exist of the leader of the Me-Wuk people at Pigliku, the Big Creek Rancheria in Groveland. Known to his people as Nomasu and to outsiders as Captain Louie, he was chief from about 1850 until his death in 1893. It is said that he encouraged his people to abandon resistance to the invading outsiders, knowing this was their only hope of survival. (Carlo M. De Ferrari Archive)

Sophia Thompson was the daughter of Nomasu. After Nomasu's sons died, he trained Sophia to become the tribal leader after his death, which occurred in 1893. Her first duty was to organize a cry for him, which included the burning and rebuilding of the Big Creek roundhouse. She passed on detailed information about the traditional ceremonies and dances of the Me-Wuk in the Big Creek area. (University of California, Berkeley.)

Two

In Search of Gold

Gold mining in southern Tuolumne County began in 1849, when James Savage, led by Native Americans of the area, discovered gold near present-day Big Oak Flat. More finds were made along creeks to the east. Together, these became known as Savage's Diggings.

After Savage left the area in 1850, the first gold camp was renamed Big Oak Flat in honor of a gigantic oak tree. Smaller camps to the east were called Garrote, a Spanish word referring to "hanging," and Second Garrote. The surrounding areas were exploited using placer mining. Big Oak Flat, in particular, boomed into a bustling town of about 3,000.

To provide water and support mining, the Golden Rock Water Company was formed by Andrew Rocca in 1855. It brought water 40 miles from the South Fork of the Tuolumne River via a system of ditches and flumes. Unfortunately, a disastrous fire in 1863 completely destroyed Big Oak Flat, which never recovered.

By the 1870s, easily exploitable gold was substantially depleted. The feverish Gold Rush was over. However, starting in the 1880s, new technologies led to a second boom in hard-rock mining, which required deep shafts dug into the earth. Numerous mills sprang up in Big Oak Flat and Garrote (Groveland) to process the ore lifted out of the shafts.

By the 1920s, this second boom also faltered due to stagnant gold prices and declining ore. By 1950, gold mining had completely ceased.

The first European American to discover gold in southern Tuolumne County was James Savage, an Illinois native who in 1848 moved to Woods Creek, where he established a trading post with Native Americans. In 1849, they led him to Rattlesnake Creek in present-day Big Oak Flat, where he started a mining camp. Another camp (today's Groveland) was founded nearby soon thereafter. Together they were called Savage's Diggings. (Bancroft Museum.)

The miner's life in the early goldfields was hard. There was no guarantee that gold would be found. The weather could be cold and snowy in winter and very hot and dry in summer. Food was often scarce. Conditions were often harsh. This photograph, taken in the early 1900s, shows a Groveland-area miner's cabin from the 1850s. (Graham Family Collection.)

News of Rattlesnake Creek's rich deposits attracted numerous gold seekers. Other adventurers came to supply the miners with their needs. The area grew rapidly into a town with a population of roughly 3,000. It was recorded to have four hotels, several bakeries, churches, a theater, and numerous saloons. In 1852, it changed its name to Big Oak Flat in honor of an enormous oak in town.

Southern Tuolumne County had substantial gold suitable for profitable placer mining. The earliest miners could easily pan for gold in streambeds. Later, as the gold gradually became scarcer, miners had to channel large quantities of water to wash the surface dirt to uncover the underlying gold. In this photograph, two miners are seen directing water from an open flume against a stream bank.

Miners became more and more inventive as gold became scarcer. This photograph shows miners using a long sluice box with earth-laden water. Riffles perpendicular to the water flowing in the box served to slow the heavier gold and separate it from the dirt and gravel, which were carried away by the water. The heavier gold tended to stay in the box for easier extraction.

By the 1860s, placer mining became increasingly difficult. Miners needed significantly more water to extract gold. They began hydraulic mining, where high-pressure jets of water were used to separate gold from the earth. As evident in the photograph, it caused severe erosion in slopes and polluted streams. By the 1880s, stricter regulations significantly curtailed its use. Today, dramatic erosion fields can still be seen along Ferretti Road. (Cecilia Crocker Collection.)

To satisfy the demand for water, the Golden Rock Water Company was organized in 1855 to get water from the Tuolumne River's South Fork and transport it 36 miles to customers. Service began in 1860. Its highlight was the Big Gap Flume, a 2,000-foot-long, 265-foot-high wooden flume to carry water across a gulch (now at Buck Meadows). Decayed, it fell in a spectacular collapse during an 1868 storm.

Moving large quantities of water over long distances was a tremendous challenge that led to ingenious technology solutions. The destruction of the elevated Golden Rock flume led local water entrepreneur Andrew Rocca to build an inverted siphon in 1869 to traverse the Buck Meadows gap. The photograph shows the large pipes carrying gravity-propelled water up and down across the gully. Portions of the pipe are still visible today.

The bulk of water supplied to gold camps and settlements flowed through open water ditches. The principal Golden Rock aqueduct followed terrain contours from a diversion reservoir at Hardin Flat to Big Oak Flat. Through its course, tributary ditches delivered water to specific ranches and mines, such as the canal in the photograph. At its peak, the system comprised over 100 miles of waterworks.

In the early 1860s, Big Oak Flat was addressing its water and ore depletion challenges. However, on October 25, 1863, a disastrous fire almost completely destroyed the town, comprised largely of wood buildings. The fire could be seen from Sonora, 15 miles away. This photograph shows the impact two decades later, with only few structures rebuilt. The town never fully recovered and rescinded its incorporation in 1864.

By the 1880s, with the emergence of better technology, hard-rock mining replaced placer mining. Miners drilled large shafts into the ground, often following veins seemingly connected to proven placer deposits. Gold-bearing rock was blasted out deep underground and then hauled to the surface for processing. This photograph shows several miners with their tools in front of the mine shaft.

The Longfellow Mine in Big Oak Flat was acquired in the 1860s by Dearborn Longfellow, a businessman from Maine. The Longfellow Mill was built in 1873 and family-operated until the 1890s, yielding 24,200 ounces of gold by 1900. The complex was abandoned in the 1910s. After a brief revival in the 1930s, mining ceased at the site in 1948. Mill ruins are still visible near Big Oak Flat.

Big Oak Flat was the site of several mines due to its level land and rich ore deposits. The Mack mine was named after Albert Mack, a German immigrant and storekeeper active from the 1850s boom. Its primary shaft was 600 feet deep. In this photograph, a group of miners is joined by several women and a dog in front of various mine structures. (Tuolumne County Museum.)

The Mississippi Mine was in the western part of Big Oak Flat. This large headframe was used to lower miners and materials into the shaft. The gray-bearded man in the rear is Rufus Keyes, one of the area's earliest prospectors. He inaugurated mail service to the area in the 1850s. He also operated a transport business along Big Oak Flat Road. (Tuolumne County Museum.)

Several mines and mills operated near Big Creek, three miles east of Groveland (close to present-day Pine Mountain Lake). Because of its local water source, it was an early placer mining center. Later, it also developed hard-rock mines and mills. This photograph shows a stamping mill with the flume carrying water to the wheel powering mill operations. A woman can be seen in front of the mill. (Tuolumne County Museum.)

Groveland also had numerous hard-rock mines. The Del Monte Mine was southeast of the town center. This photograph shows the stamp mill and headworks. It closed in 1906 but briefly reopened in 1921. After its closure, Groveland tapped the mine for town water despite the water being so iron-laden that it could "change a sheep's wood red," as the locals said.

The Gold Ship Mine was one of several between Groveland and the Tuolumne River. It began production in 1913. The deposit was opened for a width of 80 feet and was several feet thick. The associated roller mill ran at full capacity, and gold content was high. William J. Graham was its owner and manager. This mine office was on the property. (Graham Family Collection.)

The Hull Mine was another mine northeast of Groveland. It was situated near the present-day Clements Road. It was in operation in 1903 under the supervision of W. Vincent. This photograph shows the adit, the horizontal entrance to the mine. (Graham Family Collection.)

26

The area around the Gold Ship Mine included a number of other mines, such as the Duleek and Kanaka Mines. William Graham, who owned the Gold Ship, lived in this house nearby as part of the Gold Ship Grounds. Once mining ceased, the property became a turkey farm and eventually a cattle ranch. Today, the subdivided area is known as Graham Ranch. (Graham Family Collection.)

The Two Brothers Mine was in Big Oak Flat near today's Harper Road. Records suggest it was not far from the Mack and Little Sisters Mines. This 1930s photograph shows the narrow-gauge tracks leading past the mine's primary tunnel. Like other nearby mines, operations appear to have ceased by the 1940s. The mining boom was over in southern Tuolumne County.

The deep shafts of hard-rock mines had to be serviced from the surface by long vertical shafts called lifts. By the early 1900s, these lifts were powered by portable steam engines. This photograph shows one such engine (on the right) as well as two men (on the left) guiding a bucket above a shaft near the Gold Ship Mine. (Graham Family Collection.)

When mechanical equipment and power were unavailable, mine tasks had to be done by miners. The work was very physically demanding. Miners often suffered injuries and even death from mining accidents. Here, two miners work above a vertical shaft on the Gold Ship property. (Graham Family Collection.)

Three

TRAVELING THE BIG OAK FLAT ROAD

Groveland and Big Oak Flat have always been closely linked to the wonders of nature around them, especially Yosemite. Soon after the first sighting of Yosemite Valley by non-natives in 1851, news of the region's wonders spread, bringing the first sightseers. President Lincoln signed legislation in 1864, in the midst of the Civil War, making Yosemite Valley the first lands in the nation set aside for "public use, resort, and recreation."

By 1874, a primitive toll road was completed from Priest Station enabling visitors to reach Yosemite Valley. By the late 1800s, travelers could take a train to Chinese Camp, then board a stage for a 60-mile trip to the valley. On the way, they passed through Big Oak Flat, Groveland, and Second Garrote and a series of toll stations along the route—Priest, Smith, Hamilton, Colfax, and Crocker—and other wayside stops. These stations offered an overnight stay, a meal, and fresh horses. Accommodations could be as simple as tents with campfire meals or well-developed resorts with comfortable beds, fine meals, and outdoor recreation. Development of some of these places, and transportation to and from them, was often by Groveland-area residents.

Tourism entrepreneurs promoted attractions along the way, such as the Hangman's Tree and Rainbow Pool, to lure people to travel the Big Oak Flat Road to Yosemite rather than a competing road to the park.

By the early 1900s, motorcars were replacing actual horsepower. This necessitated better roads. One improvement was the construction of the less-steep new Priest Grade to reach Big Oak Flat and Groveland. Tourist traffic increased steadily through the years, making Highway 120, the old Big Oak Flat Road, the leading access road to Yosemite. Providing for travelers' needs helps keeps the Groveland area vital.

Tourism has played a leading role in the economy of the Big Oak Flat–Groveland area since Yosemite became a park in 1864. The completion of the Big Oak Flat Road to Yosemite Valley in 1874 increased travel and development along its route. This photograph shows the steep zigzag section of the road that gave early tourists access to their valley destination. (Celia Crocker Collection.)

Travelers must ascend 1,600 feet from Moccasin Creek to reach the top of Moccasin Hill. Early miners used a mule trail that climbed steeply up its spine. By 1859, Grizzly Gulch Wagon Road (Old Priest Grade) replaced the trail. Early automobiles demanded a less steep grade. A new road was completed on the opposite side of the gulch. New Priest Grade is seen before its 1925 paving. (Eaton Family Collection.)

Touring wagons were often used to take visitors along the Big Oak Flat Road from Chinese Camp to Yosemite. Forrest Lumsden, whose brothers were road and bridge builders in the area, stands at the far left end of his touring wagon. For a number of years, the Chinese Camp livery was owned by John Adam Gray of Groveland.

In the 1870s, Big Oak Flat and Coulterville formed competing toll road companies. They vied to be the first to complete a wagon road into Yosemite Valley. In 1874, the Coulterville Road was completed 29 days before the Big Oak Flat Road, but the latter quickly predominated. Here, men wait for the stage with a sign showing toll rates around 1912. (Tuolumne County Museum.)

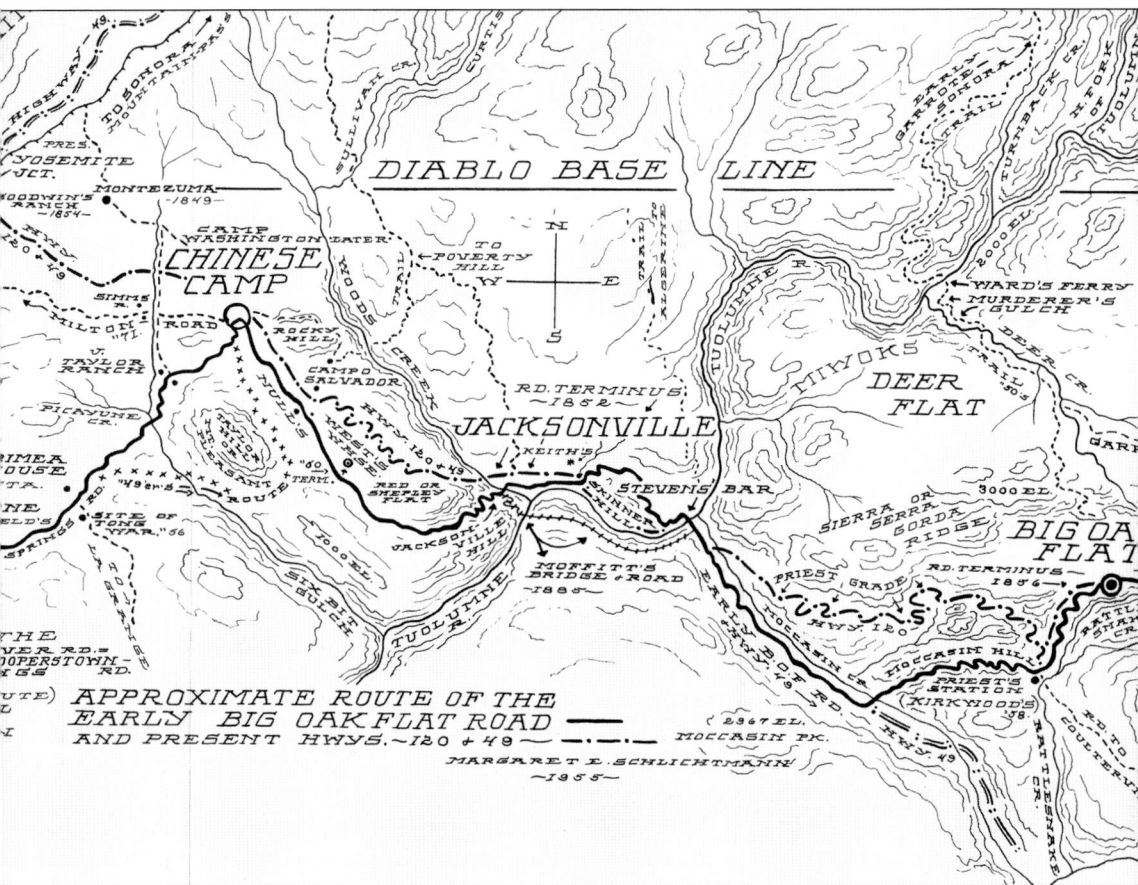

This map was drawn by Margaret Schlichtmann for *The Big Oak Flat Road to Yosemite*, cowritten with Irene Paden. It shows the approach from the west to Moccasin Hill and the roads to Big Oak Flat and Garrote (Groveland). It also shows the early trails to mining areas and to Sonora from Big Oak Flat and Jacksonville. The town of Jacksonville was well known for mining and William Smart's orchards, gardens, and nursery. His oasis provided much-needed produce to the early miners and settlers for miles around as well as to travelers passing through. Jacksonville has lain under the waters of Don Pedro Reservoir since 1971. (Awani Press.)

In 1853, Alexander and Margaret Kirkwood, from Scotland, purchased the miner's supply Rattlesnake Store at the top of Priest Hill. Under the Kirkwoods' ownership, it began serving travelers' needs. When Alexander died in 1870, Margaret married engineer William Priest. Priest Station became the first in a series of way stations along Big Oak Flat Toll Road. A traveling drum and bugle corps is seen at Priest Station in the 1890s. (Tuolumne County Museum.)

Priest Station, shown in 1918, was considered one of the best stops on the road to Yosemite. The Priests brought Jesse Carlaw, Margaret's niece, from Scotland in the 1880s to help run the hotel. Eventually it grew to have 22 buildings. Local John Ferretti recalled, "It was a high-class establishment and well known from one end of the state to the other, the cuisine was excellent."

In 1913, townsfolk who lived "on the hill" undertook to build a new road fit for automobile travel. Locals donated labor, resources, transport, and money to get the job done. Here, a group of volunteers from the Big Oak Flat–Groveland area digs the roadway for New Priest Grade. (Kundrotas Family Collection.)

New Priest Grade was named in honor of Margaret Priest, who promoted its need. Both Old and New Priest Grades begin at Moccasin and end at Priest Station. The longer, gentler new road enabled early cars to reach the top without overheating, which promoted car touring. Stages remained an option, as evidenced by the stage ticket office behind the gentlemen in this c. 1920 photograph. (California State Parks, permission requested 2019.)

Daniel Corcoran began working at Priest Station in 1879 at the age of 16. In 1896, he and Jessie Carlaw married and assumed most of the management of Priest Station. They became proprietors after Margaret's death in 1905. A 1926 fire destroyed all 22 buildings, including this hotel. Corcoran rebuilt on a much smaller scale. The Anker family, owners of Priest Station today, are Corcoran descendants. (Tuolumne County Museum.)

After leaving Priest Station, travelers passed through Big Oak Flat. It was a substantial town during the Gold Rush, with an 800-seat theater, many stores, and four hotels until an 1863 fire destroyed most of it. James Kenny rebuilt his Yosemite Hotel after the fire. By the time of this c. 1900 photograph, it had been lost again. It stood in the empty lot seen here just west of the Wells Fargo building. (Celia Crocker Collection.)

35

This is the trunk of the once-magnificent "Big Oak," the tree that gave Big Oak Flat its name in 1850. The undermining of the oak by greedy miners searching for gold among its roots can be seen. It was burned in Big Oak Flat's devastating fire of 1863 but remained standing with its branches trimmed for safety until 1869, when it fell.

The Big Oak crashed to the ground in a big wind. Many photographs were taken of travelers and locals amid its gigantic splayed-out roots. This photograph was taken before 1901, when another fire destroyed the fallen tree. Its charred remains are enclosed in a stone memorial near where it stood. (Bruce DeBoer Donation.)

The Schroeder Hotel, above, once served miners and travelers in Garrote (Groveland). It was on the south side of Main Street in the center of town. The Washington Hotel, later renamed the Savory, was another early Garrote hotel. It sat about where the Charlotte is located. The Europa Hotel, destroyed in a 1920 fire, was across from and a bit east of the Groveland Hotel. (Tuolumne County Museum.)

The current Groveland Hotel, built in 1850, was first a trading post and a home before becoming a hotel in 1866. The Garrote Hotel, one of several in Garrote to serve travelers, was owned by Matthew Foot, whose name is seen on the balcony sign. When Garrote changed its name to Groveland in 1875, the hotel soon did, too. It changed ownership many times through the years. (Carlo M. De Ferrari Archive.)

37

This huge oak tree in Second Garrote, just east of Groveland, was the fabled "Hangman's Tree" used to dispense 1800s-style swift justice. Promotion by area entrepreneurs made this a tourist stop along the Old Big Oak Flat Road. The tree was burned in a 1969 fire, though it had died many years previously. Today, a plaque memorializes the tree's remains.

Bret Harte's Cabin in Second Garrote, two miles east of Groveland, was a tourist attraction along the road to Yosemite until it burned down in 1969. Until their deaths in 1903, it was the home of James Chaffee and Jason Chamberlain, two beloved local miners turned homesteaders. It is believed that Harte's popular tale "Tennessee's Partner" was inspired by the lifelong loyalty of these men, but Harte was never known to visit there.

Gold's lure brought Easterners Chaffee, left, and Chamberlain, right, to the area in 1849. After mining for several years, they built a home in Second Garrote in 1862. Travelers were invited to camp on their land. An 1893 wayfarer's diary tells of their warm hospitality and the delight of camping amid their apple and pear trees. They lived in devoted friendship until illness took Chaffee in 1903. Despondent, Chamberlain took his own life. (Kundrotas Family Collection.)

Travel along the Big Oak Flat Road from the Central Valley to Yosemite involved overnight stays. Most travelers stayed at the toll stations along the way; their accommodations ranged from tents with campfire cooking to very nice inns with all the amenities. Some adventurers camped at natural spots or were invited onto private lands along the way. (Bruce DeBoer Donation.)

About 1901, the Peri Ranch became the office and home of the developers of the Tuolumne Power Company, which had purchased the Golden Rock Water Ditch. It ceased operation in 1917, when Hetch Hetchy was being developed. Judge Wesley Osborne purchased the ranch in 1946 and renamed it Sugar Pine Ranch. The Osbornes improved the house and added cabins. They housed guests and were famous for their breakfasts and chicken dinners.

This large meadow was George Sprague's Ranch. In 1871, he partnered with homesteader John B. Smith. Their 5,000-square-foot barn served as a relay station, providing fresh horses for stages traveling the Big Oak Flat Road. It had dual entry and exit ramps for stages. Feed hay was harvested from the meadow. Smith Station provided accommodations and meals for stage passengers, including Teddy Roosevelt. (Nicolini Family Collection.)

Hamilton Station, another rest stop on the Big Oak Flat Road, was built by Alvah and Johanna Hamilton around 1892. It was located where the road to tourist attraction Bower Cave met the Big Oak Flat Road. This location helped make the resort a big success. George Bartlett, 1920s owner and guide for Hetch Hetchy survey parties, renamed the area Buck Meadows. He held rodeos and polo matches there. (Tuolumne County Museum.)

James Ackerson is shown here sitting at Elwell's Toll Station. Charles Elwell, an early area miner, built a watering stop in the mid-1860s at a reliable source of water, Colfax Spring. It became a toll gate on the Big Oak Flat Road. The toll station was later moved to the current Rainbow Pool area. (Tuolumne County Museum.)

In 1874, James and David Lumsden built a covered bridge to span a narrow rocky canyon above a waterfall on the South Fork. Colfax Spring Toll Station was moved there, and paying a toll was inescapable. John Cox, who built a cabin on a large rock above the waterfall, was toll-taker for 20 years. This is today's popular Rainbow Pool. (Nicolini Family Collection.)

The Cliff House sat perched on a rock ledge above Rainbow Pool. The toll keeper's cabin once located there became the nucleus of the early Fall Inn. By the 1920s, the Cliff House Inn and cabins along the river were a popular tourist stop. It was rebuilt after a 1939 fire, but a 1958 fire saw its demise as a resort. It remains a popular swimming hole. (Thomas Family Collection.)

The Old Mine Cocktail Cavern was dug into the hillside across from the Cliff House. The tunnel provided a cool and unique setting for a drink for Cliff House guests and locals. A large sign inside gave the history of the Big Oak Flat Road, which ran right past it to the bridge over the South Fork until the road was later realigned. (Thomas Family Collection.)

Crocker's Sierra Resort, built about 1880, was at the top of Harden Hill near Rush Creek. It vied with Priest Station as the most important stop on the Big Oak Flat Road. Its 40-year guest list includes Joseph LeConte, James Hutchings, John Muir, and Herbert Hoover. The photograph below shows the first Locomobiles to travel to Yosemite on the Big Oak Flat Road, stopping at Crocker's in 1901. (Celia Crocker Collection.)

43

The Carl Inn Resort was built in 1916 in a beautiful spot along the South Fork by Dan and Donna Carlon. It had a short life but was much loved by those who enjoyed camping, hiking, fishing, and swimming in the river or the resort's pool. It burned down in 1920, was rebuilt, and burned again. In 1932, Yosemite took over the land. (Phillips Family Collection.)

Travel along the Big Oak Flat Road, whether for business or pleasure, has always been a major contributor to the economy of the Big Oak Flat–Groveland area. With Yosemite National Park in Groveland's backyard, a need for lodgings, restaurants, workers, and transportation has helped sustain the area through the years. (Bruce DeBoer Donation.)

Four

They Lived on the Hill

Word of new gold strikes in the Groveland–Big Oak Flat area spread quickly throughout the region, across the country, and even around the globe. It brought thousands of people to seek their fortunes. Among the earliest were Mexicans who had lived in surrounding valleys. Their influence remains in numerous local Spanish place names, such as Sonora and Garrote.

Many early settlers came from the American East, making the arduous journey across the Great Plains and mountains. Others came by sea via San Francisco, either rounding the Horn of South America or crossing the Isthmus of Panama.

Many adventurers, including English, Irish, and Scottish settlers, arrived directly from Europe. A large number came from Northern Italy and established prosperous lives in the region. Their success can be seen in Italian names on public facilities like Laveroni Park and Ferretti Road. In addition, many Chinese miners came and prospered only to be forced to return due to ore depletion and anti-Chinese laws.

Through 1860, over 70 percent of residents were young men hopeful of mining's quick riches. There were so few women in the Big Oak Flat area that newly widowed Margaret Priest reportedly had 60 suitors in 1870. Men's desire for families and a fuller life led to an increase in women arriving as the towns grew and matured. Among these pioneers was an extraordinary number of strong women who helped farm the land and run the businesses, most while raising large families.

Descendants of many of these early families still call the Groveland area home.

Emanuella Antonini was born in Italy and moved to California around 1849. She married Luigi Marconi, and they established a general store in the Gamble building in Big Oak Flat in 1870. Widowed in 1876, she married Joseph Raggio and continued to run the store, known as Raggio's Store, until 1895. A mother of seven, she also operated a gem shop and was the local postmistress. She died in 1923. (Diane Marconi Simpson Donation.)

Elizabeth Carlon Phillips, daughter of John and Catherine Carlon, was born in 1864 and raised in Groveland. She married Josiah Phillips in 1903 and gave birth to two sons when she was in her 40s. Baby Sylvester and James, age four, are seen with her in this 1908 photograph. She died suddenly at home in Groveland in 1916, leaving her sons to be raised by their aunt Nora Carlon Mogan on the Groveland ranch. (Phillips family.)

In this photograph, the Martinez family is pictured gathered at a gravesite in Our Lady of Mount Carmel Cemetery in Big Oak Flat. From left to right, family members are Ernest, father Elias, Phillip, Della, mother Caroline, and Ray. They are standing at the graves of infant children Johnny, who died 1904, and Irene, who died in 1909. A letter J (for Johnny) is visible on one of the floral arrangements. Another daughter, Eleanor, was born afterwards. (Ray Rossini Donation.)

Pictured at her desk is Mary Wilson Laveroni (1913–2011), one of the area's most beloved community leaders for 60 years. She spearheaded bringing clean Hetch Hetchy water to Groveland, serving as director (and chairperson) of the Groveland Community Services District. She also helped found the Southern Tuolumne County Historical Society. Her efforts contributed to establishing a community health clinic and downtown park (named in her honor in 2002).

In this 1914 photograph, Alinus Cole Douglas of Big Oak Flat (then 65 years old), holding his granddaughter Winifred, is pictured along with other members of his farming family. His wife, Florence, is on the far right. He founded and operated a dairy in the town. The homestead of his wife's family, the Scofields, was located between Groveland and Big Oak Flat, where "the Scar" can now be seen. (Eaton Family Collection.)

A native Scotsman, James Tannahill came to Groveland (then Garrote) in 1850. He was the proprietor of one of Garrote's earliest stores, the Granite Store, from 1853 until his death in 1884. He became justice of the peace in 1853 and later Groveland's postmaster, running the post office from his store until 1880. Tannahill is shown with his daughter Cordelia about 1880. (Carlo M. De Ferrari Archive.)

Bachelor brothers John and Spencer McCready, affectionately called "the McCready Boys," were longtime residents of Big Oak Flat. Born in Ohio in the 1870s, they moved with their father to California and may have worked as miners and farmers in Big Oak Flat from 1900 until their deaths in the 1940s. They were skilled woodcarvers, often giving their work to local children. They were also talented musicians. (Library of Congress.)

This 1920s photograph is of Millard Merrell, a prominent Tuolumne County civic leader until his death in 1969. He began work in the Groveland mine owned by his father, Josiah. He also served as a district court judge, a county supervisor, and president of the California Supervisors' Association. He later spearheaded the formation of the Groveland Community Services District. Today's Merrell Road is near the family mine site. (Judy Penrose-Lewellen Donation.)

James and Clarissa Alexander Lumsden and family are seated before their Spring Gulch home near Priest Station in 1906. Family members had strong connections to area roads, building local bridges, roads, and trails and working as teamsters. It is not surprising that Mattie, the only girl among those nine children, is said to be the first woman to drive an automobile up Priest Grade. (Tuolumne County Museum.)

Salvador "Sal" Ferretti (1871–1946) is pictured on horseback, possibly on his ranch east of Groveland (near where present-day Ferretti Road is located). One of 10 children, Sal was the son of Italian-born Giuseppe Ferretti, who migrated during the Gold Rush. He was the owner of a successful Groveland butcher shop. Sal was a flamboyant personality known for his horses and colorful ways. (Carlo M. De Ferrari Archive.)

This 1890s photograph shows the Mecartea family before their Big Oak Flat home. In 1852, the family patriarch, James Mecartea, then 25, married Elvira Smith in Chinese Camp. They had 13 children over the next 20 years. In 1872, James moved to Big Oak Flat and opened a successful blacksmith business. After James's death in 1899, his son Austin ran it until the 1910s, when automobiles replaced horses. (Anderson Family Collection.)

Scottish-born Margaret Priest came to California in 1853, crossing the Isthmus of Panama. When her first husband, Alexander Kirkwood, died, she chose engineer William Priest out of 60 suitors. She managed their Priest Hotel near Big Oak Flat for 35 years. This photograph shows her before the hotel's Lady's Parlor, an amenity that enhanced its elegant reputation. Priest Grade is named to honor her community leadership. (Anker Family Collection.)

In this 1905 photograph, the family of Louis Cassaretto has gathered for his funeral. Cassaretto came from Italy in 1876 to help his sister run her store in Groveland. He married Adelina Bruschi of Coulterville and fathered nine children. He became a successful merchant and businessman, investing in ranches and mines. The family's two stores on Main Street are still used today, and Cassaretto's descendants still live in town. (Cassaretto Family Collection.)

Ah Chu was one of many Chinese laborers who worked in Big Oak Flat over the years. The town had a number of Chinese homes and businesses and a Chinese cemetery. Ah Chu lived in a small cabin in the Deer Flat area in the early 1900s. He was considered a kindly gentleman, often greeting local children as they walked to school and giving them small presents. (Dorel McDowell Donation.)

Sarah Ann George Gray is pictured with her first-born son, John Rufus (1875). In 1854, her family sailed around the Horn to California. About 1873, she married miner John Adam Gray, and they bought a farm in Deer Flat. John Rufus later became county constable and helped guide Teddy Roosevelt around Yosemite. Gray descendants are area ranchers and civic leaders. (Carlo M. De Ferrari Archive.)

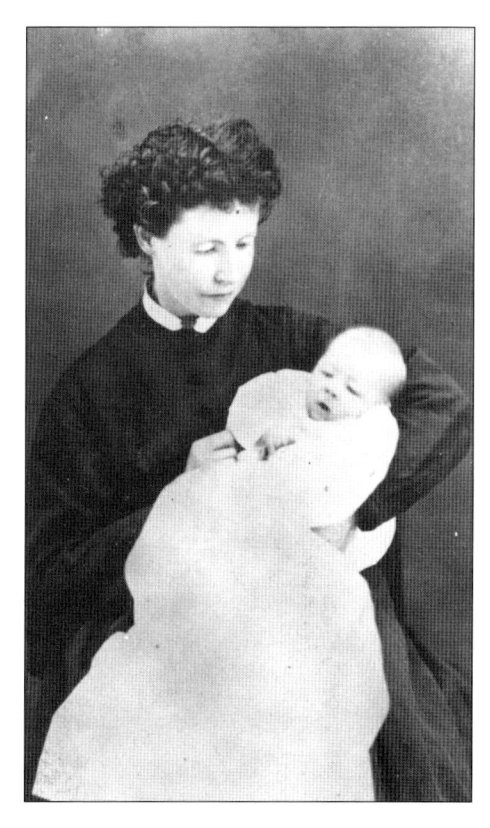

Charlotte De Ferrari was born in Italy in 1883 and came to Groveland at 16. Her father, Luigi, died in a mining accident. Charlotte had to help provide for the family. She cooked meals for locals and passersby, ultimately opening a restaurant downtown. In 1921, she opened the Hotel Charlotte, adding the next-door Gem Saloon as a restaurant. She died in 1970. (Carlo M. De Ferrari Archive.)

This undated photograph shows Edward Cobden (born 1872), a builder who came from New Jersey in 1895. He met the well-known Raggio family in Big Oak Flat, marrying Louisa Raggio in 1899. His father-in-law, Joseph, hired him to build a home for the couple. This historic house still stands in Big Oak Flat. Cobden later became a rancher, merchant, and postmaster in Groveland. He died in 1946. (Carlo M. De Ferrari Archive.)

Joseph Robert Boitano is pictured around 1900 at his marriage to Mary Carlon Meyer of Groveland. Joseph's father, Giovanni, was a successful forty-niner in Big Oak Flat. Giovanni returned to Italy, married, and started a family. In 1873, he returned to Groveland to buy a farm. He was widely known for his excellent wine. Present-day Boitano Road is near the original family ranch north of Groveland.

The photograph shows Carlo M. De Ferrari at Sonora High School around 1940. A decorated World War II veteran, author, and lecturer, De Ferrari also served Tuolumne as county clerk, auditor/controller, and official historian. Tuolumne County's archive is named for the Groveland native and now maintains his extensive collection of local historic materials for public research. Born to Italian and Scotch-Irish parents in 1923, he died in 2017. (Carlo M. De Ferrari Archive.)

This 1904 photograph shows Jacob and Jocunda Laveroni with their children George and Bernice. Jacob's father emigrated from Italy before 1860 and started a family in Tuolumne County. George was a businessman in Groveland, buying and running the well-known Iron Door Saloon. In 1943, he married Mary Wilson, who later became a prominent community leader. George and Bernice also operated the much-loved Groveland Ice Cream Parlor. (Laveroni Family Collection.)

Fifty years after the initial Gold Rush, the demands of mining and the passage of time had taken their toll on those early gold seekers. A group of old-timers gathered together in Big Oak Flat to commemorate those days in 1898. Included in the picture are, from left to right, Tom Maxey, Billy Watson, Jack Bell, George Culbertson, James Chaffee, Jim Condon, Jason Chamberlin, Barney Fox, and Jim Ballentine. (Carlo M. De Ferrari Archive.)

Daniel Carlon is seated in his packed car around the 1920s. He was the nephew of Tim Carlon of Groveland, a prosperous rancher and later founder of the Carl Inn. Daniel was also a rancher and part owner of the inn. He was reportedly known as "Dancing Dan" for his love of dancing, which he pursued despite a severe hip injury. (Phillips Family Collection.)

Five

MAKING ENDS MEET

The Gold Rush was more than gold. Many parts of the economy developed to support the communities that grew around mining. Thousands came to Gold Country to make their living in other occupations. While many came to strike it rich, they quickly realized that it was more secure to serve the needs of miners.

Feeding the communities was crucial, so ranching and farming became important. Cattle ranching was well-suited to the water-scarce region, and ranching and cattle drives continue to the present day. Other farmers turned to growing barley and potatoes and planting orchards, some of which can still be seen.

An abundance of trees enabled many to establish timber businesses. Wood was widely used in both placer and hard-rock mining as well as home building and for fuel. Wood products were vital for the construction of Hetch Hetchy. As a result, sawmills were common between Big Oak Flat and the eastern communities. Some, such as the Laveroni Mill, lasted into the 1950s.

Transportation of goods and people was also important. Before the motorcar era, many freighting businesses with large horse trains hauled goods throughout the region. To support those industries, blacksmith and wheelwright services were significant local occupations. Later, automobiles required the opening of gas stations and mechanics' shops.

Many settlers took up commerce and shopkeeping. Stores came and went, but a few lasted as community cornerstones for many years, such as the Cassaretto Store on Main Street in Groveland. It and a series of other stores successfully served the needs of local residents for decades.

Before the Gold Rush, southern Tuolumne County was largely rolling country covered with trees. When the forest was cleared and water was prudently managed, the land became suitable for ranching and farming. Many new arrivals entered agriculture to provide food for miners and other residents. In this photograph, taken east of Groveland near Crocker Station, three farmers are harvesting hay from their fields with horse-drawn wagons. (Celia Crocker Collection.)

Ackerson Meadow is approximately 15 miles east of Groveland. It is named after forty-niner James Ackerson, who sold it to cattleman Tim Carlon in the 1890s. Cattle grazed in the meadow helped feed Hetch Hetchy workers. Carlon descendants continued to graze stock there into the 21st century. In 2016, the land was purchased and donated to Yosemite National Park. (Celia Crocker Collection.)

Groveland has been involved in cattle ranching for 125 years up to the present day. Here, members of the Erickson family (descendants of the pioneer Carlon family) drive cattle from their year-round ranch in the Central Valley to summer grazing lands leased from the US Forest Service near Yosemite. The trip, with about 500 cattle, passed through Groveland and took four to five days. (Rebecca Harvey.)

From their founding, Groveland and Big Oak Flat were considered well-suited for growing fruits such as apples, cherries, and pears. Many residents cleared their land and planted orchards, selling their produce locally and across the region. On the right are orchards near present-day Ferretti Road. Many fruit trees and orchards can still be seen near the two towns. (Pratt James Family Collection.)

Many residents raised animals and cultivated fruits and vegetables for both commercial and home use. This early-1900s photograph shows brother and sister Ernie and Eleanor Martinez at their farm between Groveland and Big Oak Flat with a crop of squash. In those days, children also helped out in family food production. (Rossini Family Collection.)

Mining had a voracious appetite for timber. Moreover, most homes, ranches, and businesses were built with wood. Consequently, many sawmills were established throughout the area, starting in the 1850s. Some of the early mills, such as the Dorsey, Hobron, and Hardin Mills east of town, also supplied timber for the early water systems, such as the Golden Rock Ditch. This undated photograph shows one such mill. (Stanley Family Collection.)

This photograph illustrates the challenge of mills transporting products to market. Teamster Charles Wilkinson (on the wheel horse closest to the wheel), his wife and daughter, and two coworkers are pictured on the wagon near the Hardin Mill. Despite enlarging and moving the mill twice, Hardin lost ownership in 1884. It was later sold to local rancher Tim Carlon and the Guinn family (when it became known as Guinn's Mill). It closed in 1961. (Kundrotas Family Collection.)

A well-known sawmill was built in Second Garrote by George Laveroni, a successful Groveland businessman. It was a seasonal open-air mill producing rough-cut pine and cedar taken from the Second Garrote, Greeley Hill, and Long Gulch areas. Output was used for local construction and various customers in the Central Valley. Its crew of 10 men worked eight hours for $1.50 an hour. It closed in the 1960s. (Laveroni Family Collection.)

In addition to the area's ongoing needs, the Hetch Hetchy project led to a significant short-term increase in the demand for processed timber. One of the largest Hetch Hetchy mills was at Canyon Ranch, near the dam site. This 1915 photograph shows the sawing equipment that produced lumber for building and dam construction as well as railroad ties and bridge trestles. (HHPC.)

A spin-off of Hetch Hetchy was a mill founded by the California Peach Growers' Association. It needed a reliable source for its wooden packing crates. The association's mill on Evergreen Road near Camp Mather is pictured in 1919. A small railroad connected the mill with the Hetch Hetchy Railroad to transport products to the Central Valley. When Hetch Hetchy closed down, the association also had to stop its operations. (Ted Wurm Collection.)

This late-1800s photograph shows local freighter Samuel Bradford hauling lumber from a mill to customers. As can be seen, Bradford's team of 10 horses actually pulled two wagons of finished timber.

Until the early 1900s, horse-drawn livery was a substantial and profitable business. Many companies carried supplies, mail, and travelers throughout an area from Chinese Camp to the mining communities and on to Yosemite. This photograph pictures the Reed & Mulligan livery business in Big Oak Flat. As confirmed by the coach on the right, the livery and feed stable also served as a general stage office.

In the early 1900s, Fredrick "Rico" Cassaretto (born 1885) operated a transport business from his family's Groveland businesses to Chinese Camp up and down the steep Priest Grade. The round-trip took three days. He is shown in 1910 sitting on the wheel horse of an eight-horse team and wagon. His rig would often include another, smaller cart pulled behind the first wagon. (Cassaretto Family Collection.)

In 1901, Charles Baird established a hauling and livery business in Groveland. However, automobiles were increasing in importance—the coach sits outside in the rain, while two automobiles are protected inside the livery building. Baird later went on to operate tourist services to Yosemite in motor coaches (equivalent to today's buses). (Ted Wurm Collection.)

In 1852, miner James Mecartea married Elvira Smith in the town of Chinese Camp. In 1872, they and their children moved to Big Oak Flat and opened a prosperous blacksmith shop. It was a local landmark located on the Divide between Big Oak Flat and Groveland. When James retired, George (his eighth son) took over. The photograph shows George's Tuolumne Shoeing Shop, offering "Practical Horseshoeing." (Mecartea Family Collection.)

Gradually, Austin Mecartea, who never married, assumed responsibility for the family smithy. In addition to shop workers, the horse, and a massive anvil, this interior photograph shows rudimentary electric wires and lights. The substitution of cars for horses led to the final closing of the business in the 1930s. A series of fires severely damaged the empty building, and it was demolished in the 1980s. (Mecartea Family Collection.)

In the 1800s and early 1900s, Groveland and Big Oak Flat relied on horse-drawn coaches for transportation. Wheelwrights, who repaired and maintained wooden wheels, were vital. This undated photograph shows a young wheelwright with his tools, while others—perhaps his customers—stand behind next to a coach. A boy and a dog also watch at the right.

As cars inevitably replaced horses in the first decades of the 1900s, Groveland opened a number of garages and mechanical service shops for tourists and locals. The Yosemite Garage was on the south side of Main Street. Directly across the street (but not shown) was the Groveland Garage. (Fisher Family Collection.)

Teenager Barbara Peters of Big Oak Flat is pictured at the gas pumps at the station owned by her father, Lester Peters. This was the first station encountered by travelers after climbing the steep Priest Grade. It was also the contract station for AAA and the National Automobile Club, providing towing and repair services. (Peters Family Collection.)

Offering services to motorists and car owners was more than just selling gas. Oil change, lubrication, tire repair, and the like were all part of the business. In the 1920s or 1930s, local mechanics are seen examining a customer's engine in their shop. (Eaton Family Collection.)

As Groveland and Big Oak Flat grew, many residents became merchants and opened stores to supply community needs. In this 1930s photograph of Groveland's Main Street in the snow, the Pacific Grocery (on the left) occupies the space formerly operated as the Cassaretto Store. On the other side of the street across from the Hotel Charlotte is a meat market. (Carlo M. De Ferrari Archive.)

In addition to several other businesses, the Laveroni family also operated a store on the southwest edge of Groveland during the 1950s. Under the name Laveroni Lumber Company, it carried a complete line of building supplies, appliances, sand, cement, and gravel as well as fishing and camping supplies. "We can handle any job—big or small!!" was their motto. (Laveroni Family Collection.)

Six

DAY TO DAY

Living "on the hill," as the Groveland and Big Oak Flat population refer to their area, has always been a rich experience with diverse opportunities, challenges, and activities. Building on the area's natural advantages and their own skills and energy, the people of southern Tuolumne County created a rewarding way of life.

Raising a family was a cherished but demanding task. Early settlers established a school in Big Oak Flat shortly after the discovery of gold. Additional schools emerged in Groveland and outlying areas, almost everywhere a handful of children lived.

Enjoying the outdoors has always been important for southern Tuolumne residents, whether hunting, fishing, swimming, walking in the forest, or just exploring. For excitement-seekers, local roads also offered the chance for motorsport adventure. There were many opportunities and venues for eating, drinking, and being with friends. Women often gathered to socialize and pursue a variety of needlework.

A popular form of entertainment for the whole community was attending the local baseball team's games. Men and women alike joined community benefit organizations such as the Rebekahs and Odd Fellows to help their neighbors and to socialize. They stayed informed about local life by reading the town newspaper.

Life on the hill also brought challenges. The area's dry summers have long caused destructive fires both in town and in the forest. After a fire destroyed Big Oak Flat in 1863, Groveland also experienced devastating fires in 1919, 1920, 1933, and 1991. Forest fires repeatedly burned the surrounding area. Conversely, severe winter weather often brought deep snows that seriously disrupted local life. But these did not hamper the townspeople's can-do spirit.

A teacher poses with her students in front of the Big Oak Flat Elementary School around 1910. The first Big Oak Flat school had been built in the 1850s to serve the booming mining town but was reported to have been washed away by uncontrolled hydraulic mining. It was replaced by this schoolhouse, located near present-day School Street. This is now a residence. (Capson Family Collection.)

Small schools also served children in outlying areas from Hell's Hollow to Spring Gulch (present-day Priest-Coulterville Road). For many years, the mining and ranching area of Deer Flat north of town also had a small school. This photograph from the 1880s shows Deer Flat teacher Nellie Goodnow with children from several well-known local families, including Gray, Corcoran, and Simmons. Due to declining enrollment, the school closed in 1925.

Garrote (Groveland) had its own school, built in 1867 east of the Divide to serve students in grades one through eight. It was known as the little red schoolhouse. In 1914, when Groveland became headquarters for the Hetch Hetchy project, the old Groveland schoolhouse was inadequate. Voters approved bonds to fund a new building. The new school is seen under construction around 1915. (Carlo M. De Ferrari Archive.)

This late-1910s photograph shows local students on the steps of the new Groveland School west of town. It still only served students from first to eighth grade. It was used until the late 1960s, when it was replaced by Tenaya School. The building is now a bank. (Kundrotas Family Collection.)

Before 1992, when Tioga High School was built in Groveland, students from grades 9 to 12 were bused to Sonora Union High School, 27 miles away. The bus left Groveland and Big Oak Flat at 6:30 a.m. and returned at sunset. The journey on curvy mountain roads required one and a half hours each way. In addition, as shown here in the 1930s, the buses could sometimes get stuck in heavy winter snows. (Eva Questo Donation.)

Students of the Big Oak Flat School eat lunch in the cafeteria. The school lunch program was launched in the mid-1950s to provide meals to pupils from both Groveland and Big Oak Flat, who previously brought their own food to school. The cafeteria was housed in a separate building adjoining the school. Effie Piltz, a local homemaker, was the primary cook. (Osborne Family Collection.)

This c. 1920 photograph shows locals George Laveroni (at the wheel) and Frank De Ferrari (left front) with two friends. The rifle suggests a possible hunting excursion. Hunting was very popular in southern Tuolumne County. Deer were hunted from Big Oak Flat to Yosemite Park, where hunting was prohibited. Rabbits and squirrels were also common targets. Meat from these animals was often eaten by local families. (Carlo M. De Ferrari Archive.)

With its agreeable climate and undulating forested terrain, southern Tuolumne County has always been an attractive area for outdoor walks. In the early 1900s, a young woman walks her dog as she crosses a small stream on a footpath near the Gold Ship Mining District, about four miles north of Groveland. (Graham Family Collection.)

During the Depression, motorcycles provided economical transportation as well as a way to enjoy the outdoors. Joe Ferretti Jr. is on a 1926 Harley-Davidson owned by his friend Harold Eaton. Joe was the third generation of the Ferretti family, who owned substantial ranches east of Groveland. His father died in the flu epidemic of 1918, leaving Joe and his mother to work on the family farm. (Eaton Family Collection.)

Brother and sister George and Bernice Laveroni are seen inside their Laveroni Ice Cream Parlor on Groveland's Main Street. It was built by George in 1921, after a fire had destroyed a previous shop. Bernice managed the business. Milk for the ice cream came from the family dairy located nearby. The parlor was a town favorite until 1941, when the dairy closed and the business was sold. (Kundrotas Family Collection.)

The Mueller brewery was one mile east of Groveland. Built in 1853 by Ferdinand Stachler, it was bought by German-born Eugene Mueller in 1865. The business brewed and delivered beer and ale to local camps and even across the Sierra Nevada. Patrons also enjoyed drinks under the shade of nearby trees. Mueller died in 1906, and the brewery closed in 1911. (Tuolumne County Museum.)

Three revelers are pictured in front of the Groveland Opera Hall, across from the Groveland Hotel. Built in 1859 by businessman Matthew Foot, it was the largest public building south of the Tuolumne River. It was a popular venue for meetings, dances, music, and all forms of entertainment (including early movies). Destroyed by a 1919 fire, it was rebuilt quickly for entertainment for Hetch Hetchy workers. (Carlo M. De Ferrari Archive.)

This photograph from the mid-1880s shows a gathering on the croquet ground behind the Savory Hotel in east Groveland (near the present-day Hotel Charlotte). Among the players are members of the Cassaretto, Jones, Martin, and Laveroni families. The hotel was formerly the Washington Hotel until bought by Ben Savory in 1866. It also served as the town's telegraph office after services began in 1874. (Carlo M. De Ferrari Archive.)

Prosperous men in Big Oak Flat enjoyed a range of entertainment. In the early days, this included dancing and gambling halls, saloons, and "fandango houses," which sometimes strayed into illicit activities. The Club offered the sedate diversion of billiards. Pictured in 1897 are, from left to right, "Dutch John," Jack Wivell, "Dutch Charley," Louis Marconi, Joe Musante, Charles Decker, and Charles Doherty. (Diane Simpson Marconi Donation.)

Ten women in Big Oak Flat display their needlework handicraft. A young boy can also be seen next to a wicker baby pram on the left. Embroidery was a popular activity for Tuolumne County women of the era, either singly at home or in a group where they could socialize with friends. Clothing and home linens were often decorated by needlecrafts. (Harold Eaton Collection.)

The 1920s were a prosperous time in America and Groveland, which was in the middle of the Hetch Hetchy boom. The July 4, 1922, parade marches down Groveland's Main Street as patriotic residents watch flag-draped cars pass by. The prominent two-story Hotel Baird (later dismantled) was on the south side of Main Street near today's community hall. (Carlo M. De Ferrari Archive.)

This 1892 photograph shows Groveland schoolchildren preparing for a patriotic celebration of the 400th anniversary of Columbus's voyage to America. Perhaps due to encouragement by the local Italian community, Groveland–Big Oak Flat was the only school district in Tuolumne County to celebrate the day. The event featured a parade up Groveland's Main Street to the schoolyard, a flag raising, and patriotic speeches. (Carlo M. De Ferrari Archive.)

Lennan Lane of Groveland is pictured around 1915 on Main Street with Bruno, a black bear adopted by the town as its mascot. He was rescued as a cub by Floyd Cassaretto, who lived in the house in the background. He was the mascot for the Groveland baseball team. Bruno also engaged in staged bear wrestling matches with Cassaretto, which were popular with visitors. (Carlo M. De Ferrari Archive.)

Baseball became increasingly popular across America in the late 1800s. This 1899 photograph shows the Groveland baseball team, comprising players from the area. The two young observers are Frank (left) and Fred (right) De Ferrari. Relatives Henry and Richard De Ferrari are among the players. The Groveland team competed against nearby towns. Baseball games were popular social events featuring dinners and dancing followed by the game. (Carlo M. De Ferrari Archive.)

Big Oak Flat's Independent Order of the Odd Fellows (IOOF) lodge was founded in 1860. The IOOF was a leading men's fraternal organization during the Gold Rush era. It provided a range of services to members—miners and other working men—and their families, such as education and burial assistance. Around 1895, members of Lodge 97 pose in front of the hall. (Carlo M. De Ferrari Archives.)

This 1949 photograph shows members of Rebekah Lodge 259 of Big Oak Flat. The Rebekahs were a sister organization to the IOOF, providing charitable services to the community as well as social connections for members. In 1851, the IOOF became one of the earliest male fraternal organizations to admit women. Only 12 years later, the Rebekah Lodge was founded in Big Oak Flat.

The Foresters was a mutual benefit organization active in Gold Country in the late 1800s. Founded as a "friendly society" in Britain, it moved to North America in 1874 and grew to over 250,000 members by 1906. It pioneered insurance services to working-class members. The Foresters lodge in Groveland, pictured here, included many well-known citizens among its members, including the De Ferrari, Laveroni, and Boitano families. (Tuolumne County Museum.)

This advertisement from Groveland's *Prospector* newspaper in 1906 shows the range of goods and services advertised and available to readers as well as some of the well-known businessmen of the day. The Groveland Hotel and Bar and the Gem and Pioneer Saloons (owned by H.M. De Ferrari) were popular hospitality venues. The Cassaretto Store on Main Street, owned by Leo Cassaretto, offered a wide variety of goods to the community.

Southern Tuolumne County generally has a moderate winter climate, with roughly 31 total inches of snow on average. However, residents are always prepared for unusual snowstorms that can substantially disrupt life. This 1935 photograph shows the effect of a reported 32 inches of snow on Main Street. Pictured behind the snow piles is the Groveland Garage and Service Station on the south side.

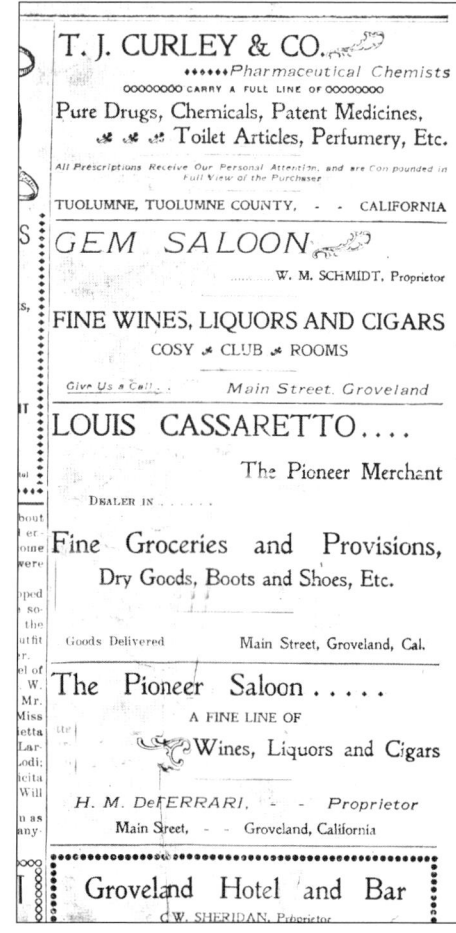

81

Hot, dry summers and abundant fuel—both wood buildings and forests—made fires an ever-present threat. Big Oak Flat was razed by fire in 1863. Groveland also experienced many serious fires. On June 3, 1933, a fire reportedly began in the Ferretti Garage (middle of photograph), which was destroyed in the blaze. This photograph was taken by Byron De Ferrari with his Brownie camera. (Carlo M. De Ferrari Archive.)

The June 1933 fire burned businesses on two blocks of Main Street, including the Ferretti Garage, a boardinghouse, and a barbershop. It also consumed several cottages behind Main Street. While it started when a truck struck a gas tank, it was said that a bootleg still might also have ignited. This photograph shows men gathering near burned-out shells of buildings (behind the telephone pole on the right). (Carlo M. De Ferrari Archive.)

Seven

ROADSIDE HISTORY

Groveland and Big Oak Flat have a number of historic buildings that provide a glimpse into their past. Visitors can still see many of these structures along Highway 120, the main road that passes through these communities.

First settled after the discovery of gold in 1849, Big Oak Flat had over 200 buildings by the 1860s. The transitory nature of gold mining and extensive forests nearby meant most early buildings were constructed of wood. That made them especially vulnerable to fire. A disastrous conflagration in October 1863 devastated nearly the entire town. Most surviving structures, including the IOOF and Gamble (Wells Fargo) buildings, were made of stone. Though some businesses and homes were rebuilt, Big Oak Flat never fully recovered.

Groveland, also settled about 1849, grew more slowly to become the larger town on the hill after the fire that destroyed Big Oak Flat. It too experienced ruinous fires in 1919, 1920, 1933, and 1991, all of which destroyed large sections of the town.

A number of old structures remain throughout Groveland, including four adobe buildings from the earliest years and the c. 1852 Granite Store, later converted into the well-known Iron Door Saloon. Several public facilities such as the jail also survive. In addition, several turn-of-the-century frame homes are still standing, some converted into shops or tourist accommodations.

In the 1910s and 1920s, the Hetch Hetchy project contributed to renewed construction in Groveland. In those years, some historic buildings were lost in blazes, but major additions were also made. Among them were the new Groveland School, the Charlotte Hotel, and a substantial annex to the Groveland Hotel.

The first Independent Order of Odd Fellows lodge was destroyed in the 1863 Big Oak Flat fire. The IOOF then acquired two abutting single-story buildings, seen here, and cut a doorway linking them. In 1924, a second story was added, creating the building that exists today. The early lodge aided families of members who were injured or died. Lodge 97 disbanded in 2017. (Library of Congress.)

This Queen Anne house in Big Oak Flat was built in 1900 for Joseph Raggio by Edward Cobden. The Raggio family had mining interests and ran a store in the stone Wells Fargo building next door. The Cobden family gifted this home to the Southern Tuolumne County Historical Society, which has been working on its preservation. (Diane Marconi Simpson Donation.)

The Gamble building, seen here, was constructed no later than 1852. Mine investor and merchant Alexander Gamble was its first owner. He rented the three commercial suites within the building to a variety of businesses. It was home to Big Oak Flat's first post office and Raggio's general store. The Wells Fargo Express Office occupied the eastern suite until 1893. A smaller stone building abutting the west was possibly the town's second jail after the first one burned down. A frame building also added to the west was thought to be an apothecary and a shoemaker's in early years. In 2007, the Cobden family gifted the building to the Southern Tuolumne County Historical Society. The nonprofit has been working on its preservation since acquiring it.

The Miner's Resort opened in 1925 as general store. A stone building next door was the beginning of the area's first auto court. In the early 1950s, the post office was moved to the Miner's Resort from the Robert L. Smith Store. It became a restaurant and produce mart in the 1970s. A major fire nearly reached it in 1991, but it survived. (Judy Penrose Lewellen Donation.)

Big Oak Flat's first school was built in the 1860s near the Divide Cemetery. It closed when Garrote built a school just to the east around 1867. This school was built to meet the influx of families during the 1890s hard-rock mining boom. Its students pose in 1910. When the school closed in the 1960s, the building became a residence. (Kundrotas Family Collection.)

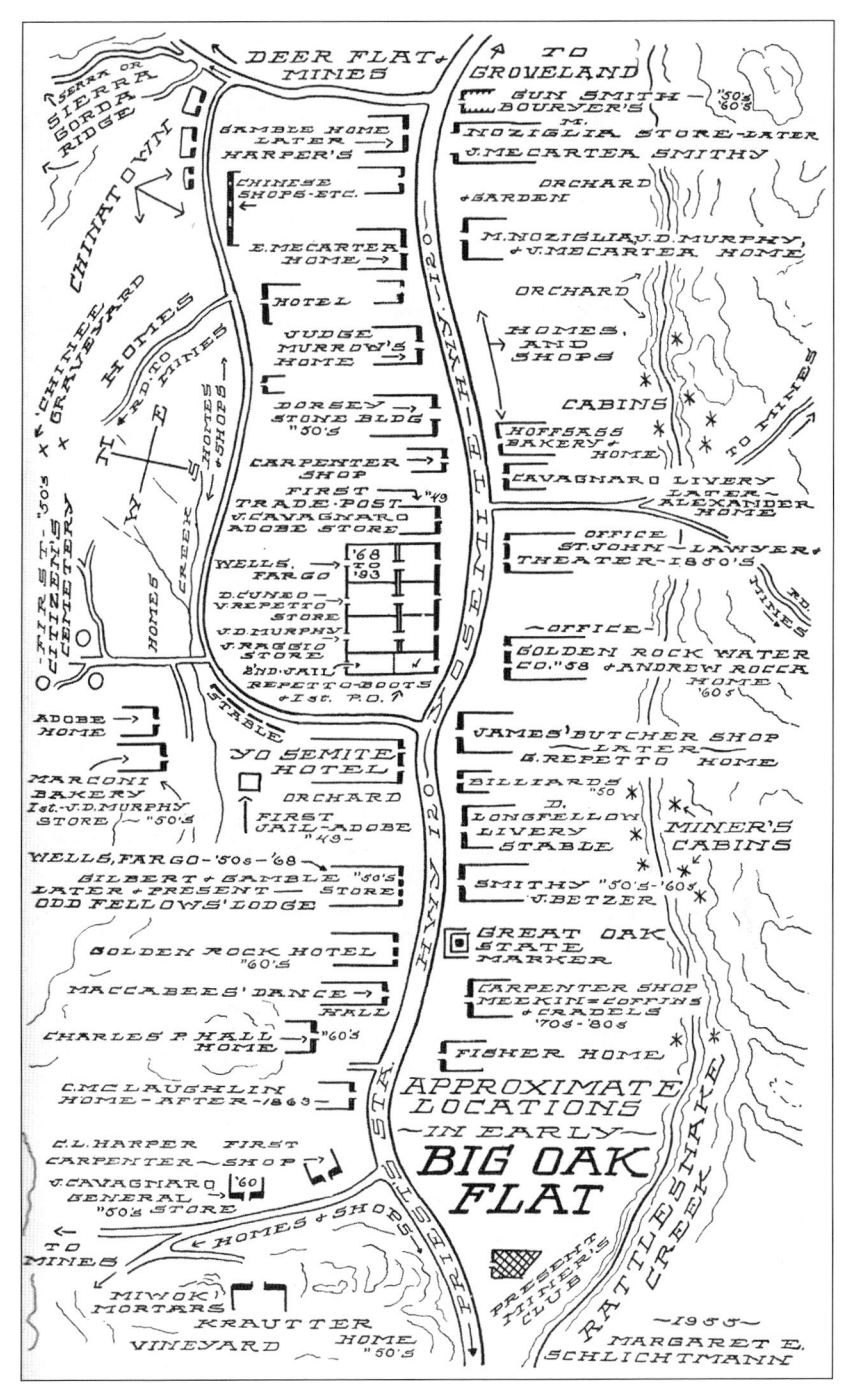

This map was drawn by Margaret Schlichtmann for *The Big Oak Flat Road to Yosemite*, which she and Irene Paden wrote in 1955. It shows the many businesses and homes in Big Oak Flat in its brief heyday, before the 1863 fire destroyed most of the structures in town. Its namesake Big Oak, Me-Wuk bedrock mortars, Chinatown, and the IOOF and Wells Fargo buildings can all be found. Rattlesnake Creek was the site of the first gold discovery in the area, which led to the settlement of the region. (Courtesy of Awani Press.)

Our Lady of Mount Carmel Church, built in 1861, sits atop a hill overlooking its cemetery and Big Oak Flat. When the 1863 fire destroyed most of the town, this wood-frame church was spared. About 1900, it was heavily damaged in another fire. A pasta dinner was held, and volunteers repaired the damage. It continues to provide a place of worship today. (Carlo M. De Ferrari Archive.)

This home was a church on the Divide in 1900. The church closed, and Elias Martinez bought the building in 1906. Martinez and his sons removed the steeple, dismantled it, and reconstructed it as a home on the family's 1880 homestead property. A porch, sunroom, and stairs were added in the 1930s. Descendants have nursed the fruit trees and 100-year-old grape vines into production again. (Rossini Family Collection.)

Joseph and Fred De Ferrari had the Harper brothers build this Craftsman home for their parents, Augustine and Maria, in 1917. It sits on Old Deer Flat Road beyond the De Ferrari Ranch gateway. After their parents' deaths, the bachelors remained in the home. Fred managed the family dairy. Joseph was Groveland's justice of the peace. The Hansen family later lived in the home. (Carlo M. De Ferrari Archive.)

When Margaret Lenan Coyle was widowed in 1867, she became a housekeeper for Robert Simmons to support her five children. She married Robert in 1869, had four more children, and was widowed again in 1892. Margaret's sons had this house built for her around 1900 by Edward Cobden. Her home is now a bed-and-breakfast. (Eva Questo Donation.)

In 1893, Jacob Laveroni married Jocunda Boitano. They purchased this house, built in 1877, and acreage on Main Street in Groveland. Jacob made improvements to it and built a nearby barn around 1920 for the dairy business they ran until the mid-1940s. The property, now Mountain Sage, is still in the family. (Tuolumne County Museum.)

Henry De Ferrari had this cottage built for his bride, Rose Cassaretto, in 1899. It is said that Rose's father prevented the couple from eloping at an earlier date. He told Henry that Rose was too young to marry but that he could marry her when he could build her a house. In the late 1980s, this house was saved from demolition by being moved slightly and made part of a Groveland shopping plaza. (John Stone Donation.)

This adobe, considered the oldest building in Groveland, was the site of the first trading post owned by Casimer Raboul around 1850. It became the Cassaretto Store in the 1870s. Louis Cassaretto built the east annex in 1904. Later, the original store became the Red & White Store and Tiano's, and it is currently a thrift store. The annex became the Groveland Justice Court and then a Mexican restaurant. (Stanley Family Donation.)

By 1898, the Cassaretto Store was doing so well that Louis Cassaretto hired Edward Cobden to build an adjacent house. The family moved from the upstairs of their store, where their nine children were born, into this home. By 1905, both Louis and Lena died, leaving their nine children to raise themselves. Son Frank took over the store. This home is still in the Cassaretto family. (Carlo M. De Ferrari Archive.)

91

The building in this photograph is currently the Groveland Community Hall. A grocery store is one of many roles the building has played. In 1918, Frank Cassaretto had it built as an additional Cassaretto Store during the Hetch Hetchy boom era. In the mid-1920s, Cassaretto moved, leasing his store to Clyde Smith, who ran it until the 1950s. Tuolumne County acquired the property in 1959, and the Groveland Justice Court was moved here from the east side annex of Cassaretto's original store. It has also housed the constable's office, the community services district office, and a small library. As the community hall, it is used as a meeting and events venue and serves as a resiliency center during emergencies. (Eva Questo Donation.)

The 45-degree angle on this building's corner identifies it today. Sal Ferretti moved his butcher shop to this location after a 1920 fire damaged his first shop. It had a loading dock with a grappling hook to move sides of beef. Later, it became a feed and general store, and in the 1970s, it became the Garrote Pharmacy, pictured here. (Carlo M. De Ferrari Archive.)

The Groveland Jail, the small building on the left, was constructed in 1895. In later years, it was used mainly as a temporary holding area until those jailed could be picked up by the sheriff and taken to Sonora or until troublesome drunks sobered up and could be released. (Carlo M. De Ferrari Archive.)

The Granite Store, seen here, was one of Groveland's first buildings. It was on the tax rolls in 1852 but may have been built as early as 1850. Front and rear walls of cut granite blocks gave it its early name. It was the Tannahill & Watts general store and the post office for Garrote. Its name is now the Iron Door Saloon. (California State Parks, permission requested 2019.)

The peaked-roof building on the left is one of Groveland's four remaining adobe structures, constructed in 1852. Initially, Tannahill & Watts owned both it and the Granite Store (Iron Door Saloon). Sal Ferretti's butcher shop was downstairs until a fire gutted it in 1920. Jake De Ferrari added the building between the Iron Door Saloon and Tannahill & Watts around 1917. It housed the New Hetch Hetchy Restaurant. (Carlo M. De Ferrari Archive.)

The Hotel Charlotte was built in 1921 for Charlotte De Ferrari. She first had a restaurant across the street in a small wooden building adjoining her uncle Jake's saloon (now the Iron Door). In 1927, she bought and rebuilt the Gem Saloon, adjoining her new hotel, and made the Gem her restaurant. It is said that during Prohibition, she sometimes served wine from a teapot. (Carlo M. De Ferrari Archive.)

This Spanish Revival building was constructed by Frank Ferretti. It was Groveland's post office from 1935 to 1983. Minnie Ferretti was Groveland's postmistress from 1928 until 1947. The Ferrettis lived in the postmistress's quarters in the rear until Minnie retired in 1947. After the current post office was constructed in 1983, this building served as the Hotel Charlotte's bakery, a deli, and a teahouse. (Thomas Family Collection.)

The Groveland Hotel was built around 1850. Seen here in 1902, the original building has 18-inch-thick adobe walls. In 1917, Tim Carlon, one of many owners, added a large annex to the east side to provide more rooms during the Hetch Hetchy project. Through the years, it has played many roles—home, store, hotel, gambling house, saloon, ranger station, business offices, and even a bus stop. (Laveroni Family Collection.)

This 1917 photograph shows the Groveland Hotel annex, on the left, built for the influx of workers for the Hetch Hetchy project. The buildings on the right, from front to rear, are the Europa Hotel, the Tuolumne *Prospector* newspaper office, and the opera house with its awning. These buildings were lost in the 1920 fire, which also charred the front of the Groveland Hotel. (Ted Wurm Collection.)

Eight

Headquartering Hetch Hetchy

San Francisco's 1906 earthquake and fire gave city leaders the impetus to build a dam and reservoir to provide reliable water to the city. They selected a controversial site on the Tuolumne River in the Hetch Hetchy Valley of Yosemite National Park. Congress passed the Raker Act in 1913, despite a battle with environmentalists, including John Muir. It authorized the building of a dam on the Tuolumne River and construction of an aqueduct to San Francisco, 168 miles away.

Groveland's bust period, brought on by a mining decline, changed to boom when it was chosen as the construction headquarters for the project's Mountain Division. San Francisco built an administrative center where Laveroni Park is now. It had an office building, housing, railroad maintenance shops, and a hospital that treated everyone in the area.

Locals and newcomers found jobs laying track and doing maintenance work for the 68-mile railroad built to transport men, equipment, and supplies to the dam site. Some were employed as construction workers. Others provided transportation, housing, food, supplies, and weekend diversions for the huge workforce.

With the completion of O'Shaughnessy Dam in 1925 and the westward movement of construction of the aqueduct, San Francisco's headquarters in Groveland was no longer needed. In accordance with the Raker Act, all construction infrastructure and the railroad were completely dismantled by the early 1940s.

Groveland once again became a small town on the way to Yosemite and to an additional tourist destination, the Hetch Hetchy Valley.

In 1913, Congress passed legislation allowing San Francisco to build a dam in the Sierra Nevada to provide the city with water. Preservationists, led by John Muir, fought damming the Tuolumne River in Yosemite. This photograph shows the clearing of Hetch Hetchy Valley prior to flooding it. The completed project delivered water, via a gravity-fed pipeline, from the dam east of Groveland to San Francisco, 168 miles away. (Nicolini Family Collection.)

The Hetch Hetchy project was enormous. In order to build the dam and water-transporting tunnels, a railroad, power plants, lumber mills, and housing needed to be constructed first. New businesses, such as the New Hetch Hetchy Restaurant, were also needed. Beyond the restaurant are the Pioneer Saloon, the Groveland Hotel, and at the end of the street, the Hetch Hetchy administrative building.

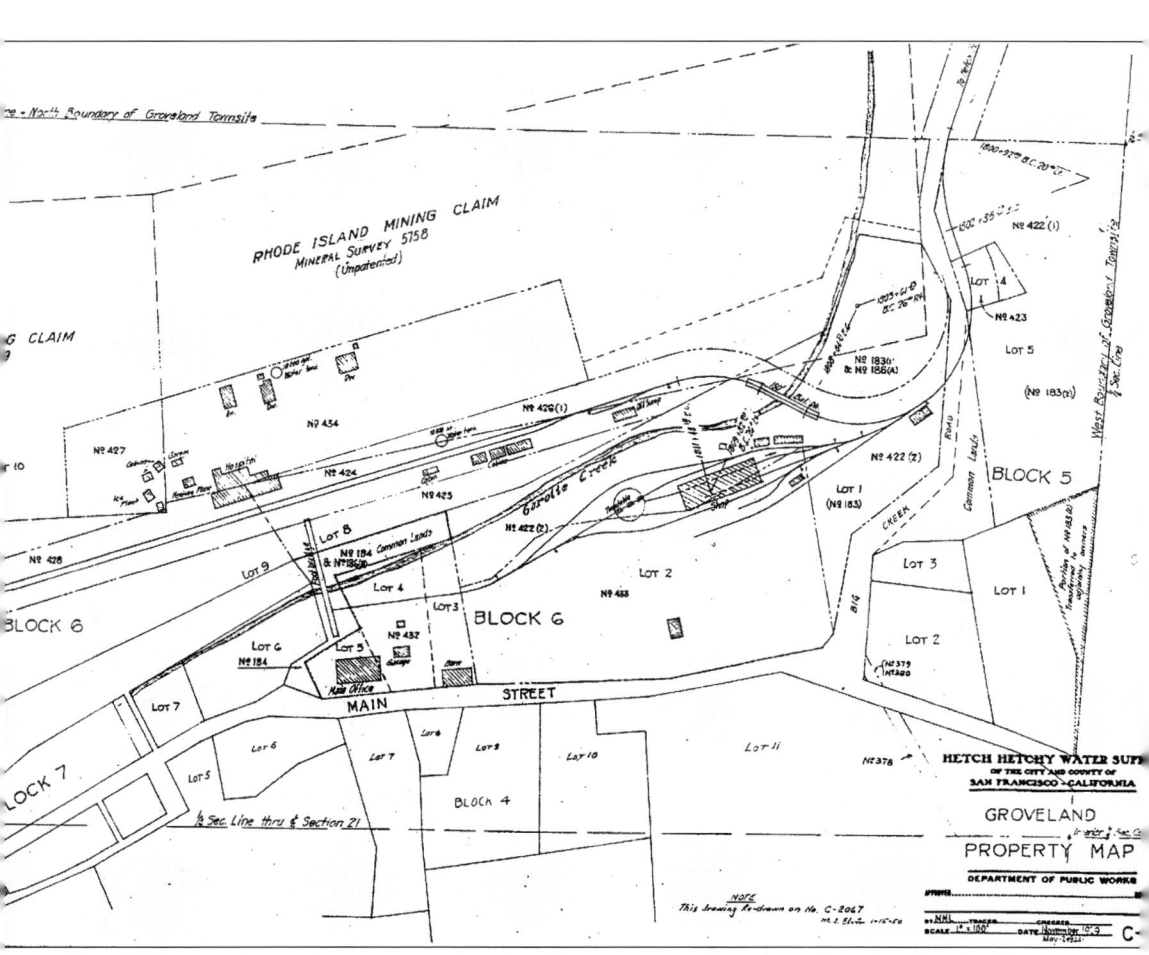

This 1929 map shows the property that San Francisco purchased in Groveland to build an administrative headquarters for the dam construction. The route of the Hetch Hetchy Railroad through the east end of Groveland is also shown. The circle in the middle marks the location of the turntable that reversed a train's direction. Groveland's skatepark is there now, and its museum and library are nearby.

This section of track was laid for the 68-mile Hetch Hetchy Railroad at Big Creek Curve, just east of Groveland. The railroad transported massive amounts of equipment, supplies, and men to remote construction locations. It connected to the existing Sierra Railroad at Hetch Hetchy Junction south of Jamestown. The railroad was constructed by San Francisco between 1914 and 1917. (HHPC.)

The Hetch Hetchy train is shown on its course through Rattlesnake Gulch, near Priest Station, after winding its long way up Priest Hill. From there, it continued its run on the hill on the south side of present-day Highway 120 to the historic mining town of Big Oak Flat. (HHPC.)

After a zigzag 1,500-foot ascent to the summit of Priest Hill, the Hetch Hetchy Railroad continued a gradual climb to Big Oak Flat. It crossed the main road from the south side to the north on this trestle near the present-day Miner's Mart. It then ran north of the historic old mining town and on into Groveland. (Ted Wurm Collection.)

The railroad needed constant repairs and new parts. This 1922 crew of mostly Groveland and Big Oak Flat–area men was employed to repair the trains at the maintenance yard in Groveland where the Caltrans yard is currently. The crew is posed on engine no. 6, a Shay, required to pull very heavy loads up the steep incline of Priest Hill. (Nicolini Family Collection.)

The railroad's maintenance yard and warehouse were located off Ferretti Road at today's Caltrans yard. The turntable, which reversed the train's direction, sat just behind these buildings where the Groveland Skatepark is today. The row of little cottages in the background was located along Main Street. They provided housing for administrative workers with families. (Carlo M. De Ferrari Archive.)

This machine shop at Groveland made the parts necessary for the repair of the trains. It also made components for new specialty railcars, such as the ambulance and bus cars. It was part of the maintenance yard constructed on what had been a small meadow next to Garrote Creek. (HHPC.)

Hetch Hetchy Railroad was known for its gasoline-powered track buses. No. 19 was fitted as an ambulance train running to the hospital in Groveland. It occasionally carried passengers. A sleek-looking bus, no. 24 with the engine in the rear, was built for speed and comfort. It could carry 32 passengers, often tourists, to the dam site. Dispatching and coordination of buses and trains using the same track was done in Groveland. (HHPC.)

This Hetch Hetchy train car is plowing snow just west of Groveland after a January 1930 snowstorm. In winter, snowplows were commonly used on trains, especially as the tracks went eastward into higher elevations. In 1921, the railroad obtained a contract for mail delivery to points east of Priest Station. It was also known to deliver sacks of fresh-caught mountain trout back to families in the Groveland area. (HHPC.)

In 1915, San Francisco chose Groveland to be the administrative headquarters for its Mountain Division. This division was responsible for construction of the O'Shaughnessy Dam, mountain pipelines and access shafts, and the Hetch Hetchy Railroad, built especially for the project. A men's quarters, hospital, and administrative building, all shown here, were erected at the east end of town in the area of Mary Laveroni Park. (HHPC.)

"The Clubhouse," or men's quarters, seen in 1918, sat on the north side of Garrote Creek. It housed some of the Hetch Hetchy's single employees and provided them with a much-needed area in which to mingle and sleep. It could not have been quiet though with the tracks running directly in front of it. (HHPC.)

This photograph shows the administrative building for the Mountain Division of the Hetch Hetchy project. It was located along Groveland's Main Street, slightly east of the current fire station. In photographs, it is often mistaken for the Groveland Hotel. The hotel's newer section, which was built to provide additional much-needed housing, looks very similar. (HHPC.)

This photograph shows Groveland in 1916, the year after it became the Mountain Division headquarters for Hetch Hetchy. The road through town was then a dirt road. In winter, rain and snow made it almost impossible to travel east of Buck Meadows. In the foreground is the two-room Groveland School, built in 1915 in anticipation of the dam project. (HHPC.)

Hetch Hetchy Hospital, built by the City of San Francisco, opened in December 1918. It was across Garrote Creek just north of Laveroni Park. Medical staff was on call 24 hours a day, seven days a week. Those badly injured while working on the dam or pipeline east of Priest Station were treated here. Railroad ambulance cars ran on tracks directly in front of the hospital. Locals were also served by this hospital. (Cassaretto Family Collection.)

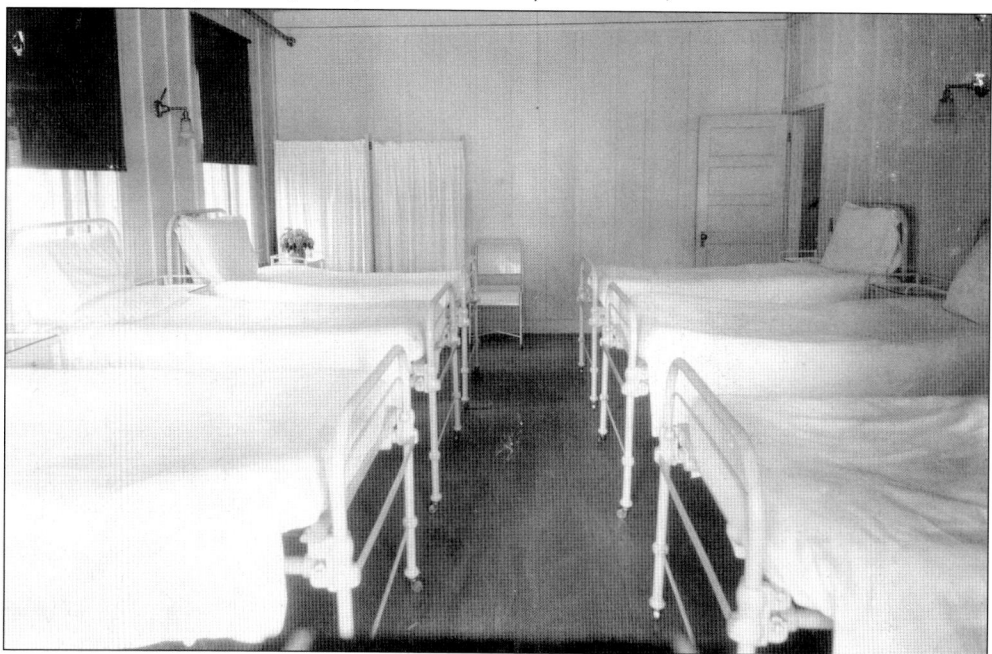

During a July 1922 fire, 30 patients were safely evacuated from Hetch Hetchy Hospital wards. Unfortunately, a young nurse was burned and suffered a broken back jumping from the building. She later died. The hospital was destroyed but was quickly rebuilt. It served the public until its closing in 1934, when it was dismantled in accordance with the Raker Act after it was no longer needed for the project. (HHPC.)

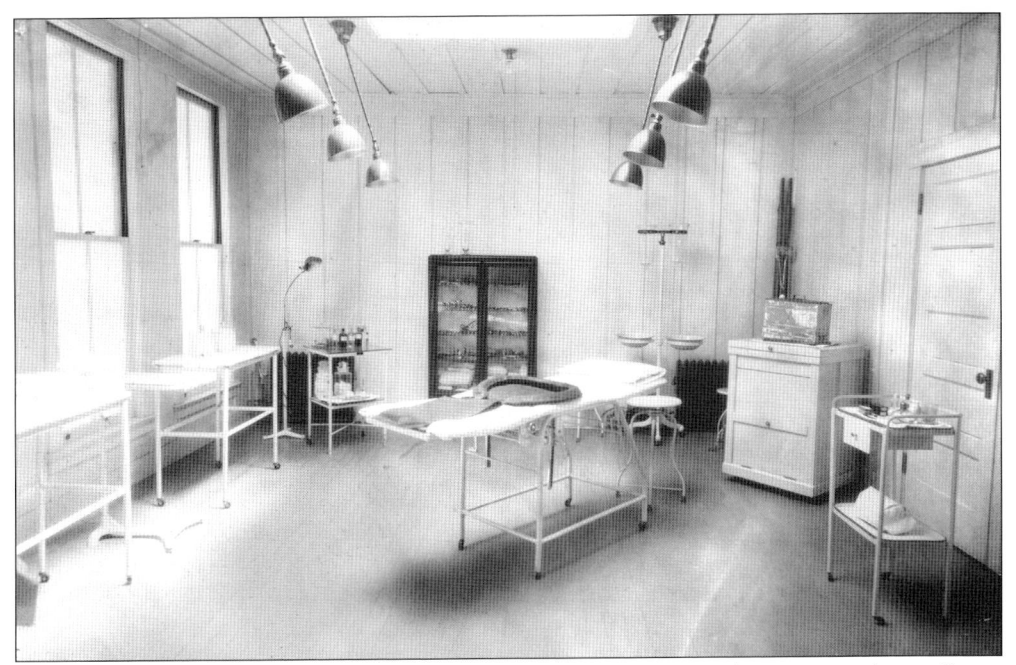

Through his years as chief of Groveland's hospital, John Degnan operated on many workers suffering very serious injuries at the dam site or other work locations. One explosion at Priest Tunnel killed three men. Doc Degnan and nurse Mary Meyer worked all night on the survivors. One lost both eyes, and another lost an arm and had a chunk of rock imbedded in his hip. (HHPC.)

Just east of Groveland, the Big Creek Shaft drops 575 feet to the main Hetch Hetchy aqueduct that carries the water on its way to San Francisco from the dam to the Priest Grade. The shaft was used for drilling the tunnel and is now used for maintenance access. Sharpening the drill bits was a constant chore done at this site. (HHPC.)

The Second Garrote Shaft, east of Groveland, is another vertical shaft built for work access on the pipeline. Drilling this shaft took from 1918 to 1923 because water gushed from it at up to 2,000 gallons per minute, flooding the shaft. Pumps were installed at multiple levels to siphon off the water. Groveland has obtained its water from this shaft since signing an agreement to buy it from San Francisco in 1964. (HHPC.)

The Baird Hotel, the third building from left, was moved from Jacksonville to Groveland to help fill the housing void that the influx of people associated with Hetch Hetchy's construction created. To provide more housing, Hotel Charlotte was built, and the Groveland Hotel added an annex. Local homes became boardinghouses, and San Francisco built small cottages on its property on the northeast end of town. (Carlo M. De Ferrari Archive.)

The Hetch Hetchy train passing through Groveland and Big Oak Flat was an exciting event for local residents. The sound of the Shay locomotive's whistle was music to their ears. It meant new buildings and improvements to the town and jobs for the area's citizens. In this photograph, locals are shown in a party-like atmosphere watching one of the early trains pass through the area they called the Divide, a 3,090-foot ridge between Big Oak Flat and Groveland on which a cemetery is located. (Carlo M. De Ferrari Archive.)

The first height of the O'Shaughnessy Dam was completed in 1923. Construction continued on the aqueduct needed to deliver water westward. The first water did not flow to the city until October 1934. This 1936 photograph shows the raising of the dam an additional 85 feet to impound more water for Bay Area use.

After the dam's completion, the Hetch Hetchy Railroad was no longer needed. Dismantling began, and the steel was sold to support the war effort in the 1940s. Here, the tracks are being removed above Moccasin. Sidings and structures in Groveland were dismantled in 1944. Some of the railway bed became roadway to access the dam. By 1949, the railroad was only a memory. (Ted Wurm Collection.)

Nine

A Lasting Boom

After completion of the Hetch Hetchy Reservoir, Groveland and Big Oak Flat resumed their quiet ways of ranching, timber, and Yosemite tourism. However, the natural advantages of a benign climate, outstanding scenery, and interesting history caught the attention of Boise Cascade, a large forest products company and vacation resort developer, as a potential location for a second-home community.

Starting in 1968, Boise began the purchase of seven local ranches comprising 3,368 acres located three quarters of a mile east of Groveland. Big Creek, a tributary of the Tuolumne River, enabled a 210-acre reservoir to anchor a planned, gated community called Pine Mountain Lake (PML). The company also envisioned an airstrip, a golf course, and a country club. The community was designed for approximately 3,500 homes. Water issues led Boise to reach an agreement with the Groveland Community Services District to provide reliable water to future homes.

In July 1969, Boise opened sales offices in the old Groveland School and in the Groveland Hotel and began selling lots. Construction of the reservoir and marina, golf course and clubhouse, and key roads all occurred simultaneously in 1969 and early 1970. Pine Mountain Lake was filled by the spring of 1970, and construction of homes began to fill the development. After completion of several phases of the project, Boise turned over management of PML to the local homeowners' association in 1974.

Today, PML continues to flourish with ongoing sales of homes and the construction of new homes. Its permanent population is about 2,800 with seasonal increases to over 5,000.

In the late 1960s, Boise Cascade, a large US timber company active in resort development, identified Groveland as a potential subdivision site. The Big Creek basin, with rolling terrain, scattered trees, and water sources, was especially promising. It had previously been the site of a Me-Wuk Indian rancheria. The 1,400-acre ranch shown belonged to R.D. Dunn following ownership by the James and Ferretti families. (PMLA.)

This is the original 1886 Ferretti barn on the Dunn ranch purchased by Boise. The barn, with its dramatic sugar pine beams, was renovated to become a sales office. It later became the Lake Lodge for resident activities, complete with a beach and boat dock. It has served that function until the present day. (PMLA.)

Boise began its sales campaign for Pine Mountain Lake prior to construction of many components of the property. This kick-off newspaper advertisement from July 31, 1969, promotes the lake as the subdivision's central attraction, despite the fact that its completion was still many months away. The advertisement's copy reads: "Imagine. A private mountain lake to sail on, ski over, swim in, and fish out of! A huge shimmering lake with over six miles of virgin shoreline and broad stretches of sun-warmed sandy beaches. This will be Pine Mountain Lake. In about a year. . . . We expect choice homesites will be gone before Pine Mountain Lake is a lake. Wait a year and there won't be anything left to wait for. The place is going to be that great. That's a promise."

The PML main entrance gate is pictured under construction in 1969. Planning, sales, and marketing for the project occurred during a period of social unrest and sometimes violent public demonstrations throughout California. The amenity of a gated community with 24-hour security increased its appeal for buyers feeling uneasy in their current neighborhoods and seeking a refuge from urban problems. (PMLA.)

To improve Groveland's first impression on potential buyers, Boise purchased the abandoned Groveland schoolhouse to serve as the PML Reception and Information Center. The schoolhouse was on the western edge of town and was the first substantial building buyers encountered when entering Groveland. As indicated in the photograph, the building was refurbished inside and out, including a new coat of bright red paint and white trim. (PMLA.)

During the initial push to sell home lots, Jeeps and Wagoneers were used to carry prospective buyers to view the development over rough terrain and around grading and building equipment. However, starting in the fall of 1969, after some infrastructure development was completed, customers could use their own cars to drive to potential lots.

This 1969 aerial photograph of Boise's reception center and parking lot indicates its easy access from Highway 120, just below the line of trees and buildings. Potential customers were offered a rest stop and free snacks. After parking their own vehicles, they were quickly driven away to see the development in off-road vehicles better suited to the project's dusty roads. (PMLA.)

Boise Cascade bought the Groveland Hotel to serve as a multiservice sales center. The building was rundown in 1969, and Boise had to remodel it extensively. It offered a reception room and sales office on the ground floor. A title company and escrow office occupied the second floor. Customers could complete nearly all aspects of a purchase on the premises. (PMLA.)

Boise also advertised PML to private pilots and aircraft owners, and it graded a dirt airstrip as part of the development. The convenience of flying one's plane to a weekend home was touted by salesmen. The photograph shows a small plane taking off from the airfield. Pilots could buzz the reception center, and salesmen would pick them up at the airstrip in a PML vehicle for a tour. (PMLA.)

The original dirt airstrip was quickly improved to an asphalted 3,600-foot runway. This aerial photograph shows PML's name painted on the runway and visible overhead. By 1971, residences and additional taxiways were built near the runway. Some owners had personal hangars, creating an air park where pilots could taxi right up to their homes. Boise Cascade transferred ownership and responsibility for the airport to Tuolumne County in 1973. (PMLA.)

Throughout 1969, earth-moving equipment like this Caterpillar bulldozer moved massive amounts of dirt and rock to construct a web of roads throughout PML. They helped create more than 30 miles of roadways along which lots were sold and houses were built. The network was later expanded to a total of 52 miles. (PMLA.)

Appropriately, Pine Mountain Drive was chosen as the name of the primary artery through the development. The photograph above shows pieces of road construction equipment excavating and grading this main roadway through the trees. Pine Mountain Drive begins off Ferretti Road at the main entrance gate and winds its way past the lake through the development. (PMLA.)

By the summer of 1969, dirt roads were crisscrossing the development. A previous Ferretti Road through the ranchlands to the northeast had followed Big Creek, whose basin was to be flooded. The new, paved Ferretti Road was created along the top of the ridge to the north of the basin. It gave additional access points to Pine Mountain Lake, the airport five miles away, and outlying ranches. (PMLA.)

This photograph was taken as the site for Pine Mountain Lake was being stripped bare, graded, and prepared for the building of the dam. For efficiency, the developers built a rock-crushing plant along Big Creek to create the aggregate needed for the dam and roads. In addition, Pacific Gas & Electric built a construction yard near the present Tioga High School and began erecting poles and stringing lines. (PMLA.)

The 210-acre Pine Mountain Lake, with six miles of shoreline, was a major part of the planned development. In the spring of 1969, Boise brought in large numbers of men and machines to begin the massive task of constructing the dam and related structures. The dam is an earth-filled structure with a downstream drainage system and a clay core. (PMLA.)

To accompany the dam, the developers needed a reinforced concrete spillway, pictured under construction. The dam and spillway structure is 120 feet high, has a 480-foot crest width, and is capable of releasing 28,000 cubic feet of water per second. It was completed in November 1969. (PMLA.)

To enable swimming and sunbathing on the lake, Boise had to bring in and dump tons of white sand at three beaches created along the shore. At the time of this 1969 snapshot, the beach areas were still barren and light-colored, in marked contrast to the darker earth on which they were laid. Later, Boise shaped and contoured them into popular lakeside amenities. (PMLA.)

Water in Pine Mountain Lake began to rise during the winter of 1969–1970. This photograph was taken near the completed dam roughly halfway through the filling process. Winter rains were unusually heavy, and the first water ran over the spillway on its way to the Tuolumne River on March 1, 1970. Currently, the average lake depth is 38 feet, and its deepest point is 100 feet. (PMLA.)

This aerial photograph of Pine Mountain Lake was taken after the creation of the lake but before the construction of homes. Other subdivision facilities were also under construction. Faintly visible at the center, jutting into the lake, is the historic Ferretti house and the barn that became the Lake Lodge. The dam is in the upper right. (PMLA.)

The lake also featured a marina next to the main beach. While lakeside homes each had their own piers, other residents could moor their boats at the marina, like this pontoon boat pulling up to the lakeside patio. Family-owned pontoon boats became (and remain) a popular way to enjoy the lake. (PMLA.)

The PML golf course is under construction in the summer of 1969. The 18-hole, par-70 course was designed by a well-known golf course architect, William F. Bell, who had over 200 courses to his credit. The 6,382-yard course is highly rated in industry rankings. The facility is now semi-private with play available throughout the year. (PMLA.)

The clubhouse, located along the golf course, is shown under construction. It is a two-story building with a deck across the full length of the second floor for outdoor dining. It was referred to as "the country club" by the developers when lots were being sold. Although the building and its facilities are open to the public, current PML residents also call it the clubhouse. (PMLA.)

The completed clubhouse houses a pro shop, snack bar, restaurant, and bar. The restaurant has a view of the golf course and the Sierra Nevada beyond. PML's swimming pool can be seen behind and above the clubhouse. Not visible are tennis courts also located near the building.

The PML pool is being built on the hill above the clubhouse and golf course. The eight-foot-deep, 30-by-60-foot pool was built for residents and guests who preferred not to swim from one of the beaches on the lake. It also provided a venue for water exercise as well as a snack shop and changing rooms. (PMLA.)

As part of its overall community development, Boise Cascade built a fire station to house both a fire truck and an ambulance. As seen in this 1969 photograph, the station was immediately outside the entrance gate (enabling services to the broader Groveland community). The building now houses the safety office for the subdivision. Responsibility for these services is now assumed by the Groveland Community Services District.

Typically, lot buyers independently contracted for home construction. Early homes on main roads tended to be smaller (including a number of A-frames like this one). Homes on the lake or with exceptional views were often larger and more elaborate. Fewer than 50 houses were built in 1969, while close to 1,000 were constructed in the decade that followed. (PMLA.)

This 1969 photograph shows the completed gate to PML, now an important part of southern Tuolumne County. It features roughly 2,800 completed houses comprising a mix of permanent homeowners, weekenders, renters, vacation homes, and investment properties. Residents enjoy PML's many amenities as well as the Yosemite–Gold Country area. Moreover, they participate fully in local organizations and activities, making substantial contributions to the Groveland community. (PMLA.)

Bibliography

De Ferrari, Carlo M. *The De Ferrari Family: Memories of Times Past*. Sonora, CA: Tuolumne Heritage Publication, 2013.
Gookin, Dave. *My Town: A Groveland Kid Remembers*. Groveland, CA: Dave Gookin, 2012.
Ortiz, Beverly R. *It Will Live Forever: Traditional Yosemite Indian Acorn Preparation*. 2nd ed. Berkeley, CA: Heyday Books, 1996.
Schlichtmann, Margaret, and Irene Paden. *The Big Oak Flat Road to Yosemite*. Fredericksburg, TX: Awani Press, 1955.
Thornton, Mark V., Judith Cunningham, Don Napoli, et al. *Big Oak Flat–Groveland: Historic Sites Survey*. Big Oak Flat, CA: Southern Tuolumne County Historical Society, 1988.
Wurm, Ted. *Yosemite's Hetch Hetchy Railroad*. Fish Camp, CA: Stauffer Publishing, 2000.

About the Southern Tuolumne County Historical Society

The Southern Tuolumne County Historical Society (STCHS) was created in 1987 by a group of local residents who were dedicated to the preservation of our area's history. Groveland and Big Oak Flat were Gold Rush towns that survived afterwards as a gateway to Yosemite National Park. The historical society decided to build a museum, which is no simple feat for such small towns. A piece of land was donated by the local water company. With intense dedication, great energy, and many donated goods and services, the museum project was under way. Ground-breaking took place in 1999 on a building that would house a museum and a branch of the Tuolumne County Library. The building was completed in October 2000 and was officially opened in May 2001. STCHS proudly continues to preserve our local history through its building preservation projects, History Resource Center, and museum archives. The Groveland Yosemite Gateway Museum is staffed exclusively by volunteers and welcomes visitors from all over the world all year long. More information is available at www.grovelandmuseum.org.

—Harriet Codeglia, President
Southern Tuolumne County Historical Society

Discover Thousands of Local History Books
Featuring Millions of Vintage Images

Arcadia Publishing, the leading local history publisher in the United States, is committed to making history accessible and meaningful through publishing books that celebrate and preserve the heritage of America's people and places.

Find more books like this at
www.arcadiapublishing.com

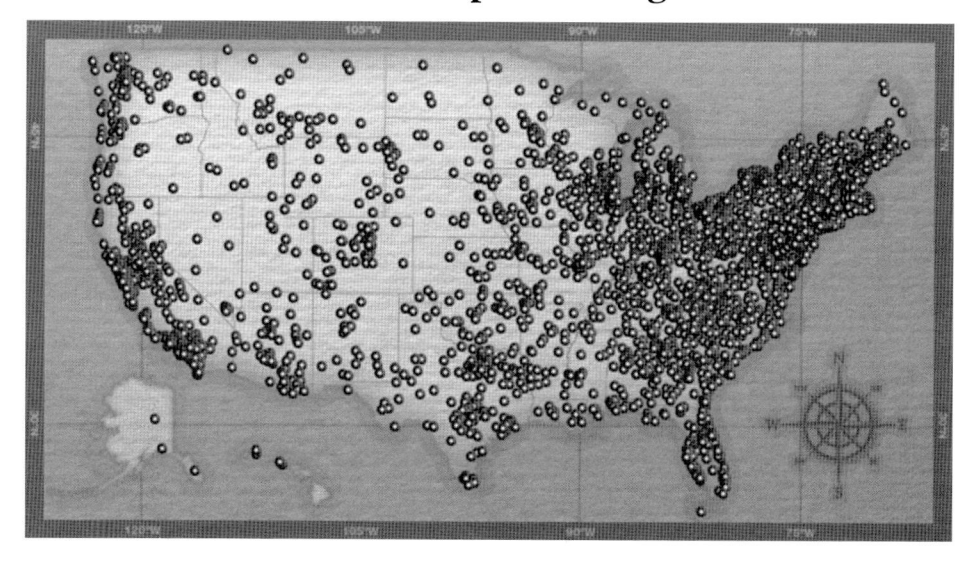

Search for your hometown history, your old stomping grounds, and even your favorite sports team.

Consistent with our mission to preserve history on a local level, this book was printed in South Carolina on American-made paper and manufactured entirely in the United States. Products carrying the accredited Forest Stewardship Council (FSC) label are printed on 100 percent FSC-certified paper.

MADE IN THE USA